THE WRATH
THE RETURN
THE TRUTH
JUDGEMENT HAS BEGUN

DANIEL OSORIO

Daniel Osorio Publications
Brooklyn, New York

**The Wrath, The Return, The Truth
Judgment has begun!!!**

Copyright © 2007, 2008 by Daniel Osorio
All rights reserved.

The biblical passages that have been included throughout this book will be in the ALT, CEV, ESV, or in the NKJV Bible version.

This Book can be ordered through ONLINE booksellers or by visiting:

www.DanielOsorio.org

ISBN: 978-1-60530-958-3 (pbk)

ISBN: 978-1-60725-959-6 (ebk)

Printed in the United States of America

www.TWRTbook.com

Note: The biblical passages that are stated throughout this book are in the Analytical-Living Translation (ALT), Contemporary English version (CEV), English Standard Version (ESV), or in the New King James Version (NKJV) Bible format.

Contents

Chapter One

INTRODUCTION

As the author of *The Wrath, The Return, The Truth*, I have felt compelled to write about the strangeness of certain events that have been taking place during our present day. These events, ranging from the fluctuations of our worldwide economy to what some have considered normal or natural occurrences, have undoubtedly increased in these days beyond what we have ever witnessed. However, the emphasis of this book is on the people, the church and its leaders, and especially religious sects. I strongly recommend that you not lose focus, set aside the importance of this message, or accept the so-called normality of these worldwide events, for they will indisputably continue to come about not only because of our government's irresponsibility, but also our own iniquities.

Although certain sections of this book may not seem to be of any concern or relevance to you, I recommend that you read its entire contents , for it was written and given in much love in order to help benefit, edify, and protect you, not only from the things that are now, but from those that are about to come. Be reassured, however, that what you will read here is the truth. For what I have written pertains to a few of the many things that I have received with regard to the present and future end-time events; I will give biblical references as evidence. So I urge that you be attentive to what you are about to read here, for it is of great importance with regard to the events that will soon take place not only in New York City but in other places throughout the world as well.

As you begin to read the first eleven chapters of this book, you will come into a series of factual events that pertain to the unusual changes that have been occurring throughout the world, the condition of the church and its leaders, and what seems to ultimately await New York City and many other places in the near future. And as you reach chapter twelve, you will read a comprehensive biblical account of the events leading up to the Great Tribulation—the second coming of Christ that many have referred to as "the rapture"—and on what point within the Great Tribulation it seems this event will take place. This chapter will provide you with an interesting and truthful insight about what many churches are omitting, or unwillingly and inappropriately teaching, in reference to the proper order of these events.

Chapter Two

THE BEGINNING

During the turn of the twenty-first century, the United States and other parts of the world began to face several unusual events that were not the norm. As most of us can recall, these events began with the American presidential elections, the catastrophe of the World Trade Center in New York, earthquakes, hurricanes, tsunamis, floods, and other changes that were taking place more often than ever before. As the frequency of these events began to increase, I became somewhat concerned, not mainly from comprehending their meaning but from acknowledging the things that are to come in accordance with what was being made known to me. In these revelations I have seen unusual and catastrophic events that are mainly described in chapter six. I know that they will take place in the near future, given the fact that others I had previously received had taken place at one time or another. I have been advised that it is imperative that I speak to the people about what is soon to come for the purpose of their protection. Nevertheless, as you continue to read these chapters, I am certain you will begin to obtain an understanding of the reasons for these constant and unusual occurrences.

As the Day of Judgment nears, these things and other major strange events will occur on the earth, especially upon the people, including those within the church because of the many sins that are being committed. And though it may seem difficult for some to accept the mere fact of a coming judgment, know that these things are evident not only in the Bible but in the events that have been taking place throughout the world in these days. Therefore, if you do consider the Bible to be the authoritative word of God, then I urge that you begin to believe and accept that what is written here is also of God, for I myself am subjected to judgment if anything other than the truth of God has been written.

Chapter Three

THE TESTIMONIAL

During my mid-twenties, I had the unfortunate experience of losing the vision in my right eye due to many years of struggling with diabetes, knowing that losing one eye to this sickness would eventually cause me to lose the other. As a couple of years passed, my vision suddenly began to deteriorate, leaving me with no other option than to go through a series of painful laser surgeries in hopes that it would prolong or prevent the loss of the other eye as well. Then, about a year after undergoing the laser surgeries, on one afternoon in August 1996, as I was driving on the Long Island Expressway in New York City, my eye gave in; I became totally blind. So I immediately activated my hazard lights and carefully maneuvered my car toward the side of the expressway. And even though I was not involved with any religious organization or activities, I realized I had a need; I remembered God and began to pray. After a few minutes had passed, my vision began to improve slightly. It wasn't enough to help guide me home, but not having any other option, I therefore decided to take the risk of driving despite the danger of not being able to see the vehicles to the front or side. My vision was just enough that I could follow the brightness of other cars' brake lights. When I finally reached home, I knew my ophthalmologist wouldn't be available, so I decided to wait for the following day.

At approximately 3:00 a.m., I woke up, and as I opened my eyes, I was surprised to find that I had regained my vision. But as I looked toward the foot of the bed, I noticed a white garment that resembled a robe; it had neither hands nor a head but stood there as if looking directly toward me. Then it turned, walked through the wall, and disappeared.

When I awoke at my normal morning hour, I was disappointed to realize that I hadn't regained my vision. When I visited my ophthalmologist, he immediately examined my eye and began to perform laser surgery to prevent the blood vessels from further hemorrhaging. But after a few minutes of doing so, he informed me that, due to the severity of my diabetic retinopathy, the eye was no longer accepting the laser, and retinal surgery would need to be performed.

From September through November 1996, I had no alternative other than to undergo three major eye operations in order to reattach my retina. During my third day in the hospital, in November, I had a dream in which I saw my aunt who had died a few years earlier, and as I attempted to hug her, she said, "Don't touch me for I haven't yet ascended to see the Father." So I asked her, "Aunt, what are you doing here?" She responded, "I came to give you a message. Read John 4:25." Then as I began to leave, I looked back and noticed that her face was somewhat disturbed but did not fully understand why. After a few years passed, I came to realize that the look on her face was caused by the many trials and tribulations she knew I would have to endure throughout the years, not only the death of my father, my blindness, losing my fiancée during the month of my last operation, and the ailments that followed, but the rejection of the messages I was instructed to give the people, especially to those within the church.

A month after my third operation, I decided to visit a church for the first time in many years, and as I sat there, a woman came and began to pray for me. To my surprise she began to quote the biblical verse, John 4:25, that my aunt had given me in the dream. Then starting a few months later, I was given two other dreams, a year or so apart. In the first dream, a voice spoke to me from heaven, saying, "There is a reason why you are alone and a reason for your condition." Then in the second dream, as I looked out my window, I noticed a man looking up toward the sky, and as he began to pray, I heard my name being mentioned in his prayer, asking about my condition. I wasn't certain about the purpose of his request, but as soon as he ended, a voice responded from heaven: "He is in this condition because I want him that way." And if that wasn't strange enough, after a few months had passed, the same message was confirmed by someone who didn't have the knowledge of these dreams.

John 4:25—The woman said to Him, "I know that Messiah is coming" (who is called Christ). "When He comes, He will tell us all things."

Exodus 4:11—So the LORD said to him, "Who has made man's mouth? Or who makes the mute, the deaf, the seeing, or the blind? Have not I, the LORD?"

Throughout the months and years, I continued to receive patterns of other unusual dreams that were coming true at one time or another, but decided to remain silent, not so much because of my partial inability to understand their meaning as because of the fear, reaction, and rejection I knew I would face if I described them. Then one evening as I was at home, I saw myself in heaven standing before someone who I believed was the Lord. And as I stood there looking downward I noticed that He was pointing toward the earth, indicating that it was imperative that I speak to the people of what was being revealed to me. As He continued to point toward the earth, I lifted my head in order to see His face, but strangely enough I wasn't able to, for as soon as I lifted my head the image switched to where I could only see His back. Then one afternoon as I visited a church, someone who didn't know about what was being revealed came to me and said, "You're going too slow; you need to speak on what is being given to you."

As you continue to read throughout these chapters, it will seem evident that these things are not normal dreams, and though I have received many types of these unusual dreams, know that of the few I have written about in this book, a couple are closely related to one another, but the majority bring out the importance of this message.

Chapter Four

WHY THE UNUSUAL DREAMS AND WHO SHOULD INTERPRET THEM

During the past couple of years I began to encounter several individuals who were having patterns of unusual and inexplicable dreams, not fully understanding their meanings or purposes but acknowledging that they hold certain spiritual significance. So in order to help others in clarifying the reason for these dreams, I have written a few biblical passages that will give meaning to them.

Although certain of your dreams may qualify as prophetic, what should be understood is that receiving such dreams does not necessarily qualify or entitle anyone to be a prophet, nor does it constitute a higher level of spirituality, for these things are obtained not by people's knowledge or authority, but by their commitment and dedication to God and the work that He has entrusted them to do in accordance to what is being revealed to them.

Joel 2:28—And it will come to pass afterward, that I will pour out my Spirit on all flesh, your sons and your daughters will prophesy, your old men will dream dreams, and your young men will see visions.

Acts 2:17-18—And in the last days it shall be, God declares, that I will pour out My Spirit on all flesh, and your sons and your daughters shall prophesy, and your young men shall see visions, and your old men shall dream dreams; even on my male servants and

9

female servants in those days I will pour out my Spirit, and they shall prophesy.

To those who are having patterns of unusual dreams: my years of experience and observation tell me that there has been a misleading belief by certain individuals, especially within the church, that a person who holds a high title or position within that church also has the ability, knowledge, or qualifications to interpret dreams. In essence, unless you know of someone who is able to properly interpret the meaning of a dream or understand certain aspects of its symbolism, it is advisable, in order to avoid misinterpretation or confusion, that you ask your pastor, priest, or church leader for a recommendation of an individual who is able to understand and interpret dreams.

Romans 12:3–8—For by the grace given to me I say to everyone among you not to think of himself more highly than he ought to think, but to think with sober judgment, each according to the measure of faith that God has assigned. For as in one body we have many members, and the members do not all have the same function, so we, though many, are one body in Christ, and individually members one of another. Having gifts that differ according to the grace given to us, let us use them: if prophecy, in proportion to our faith; if service, in our serving; the one who teaches, in his teaching; the one who exhorts, in his exhortation; the one who contributes, in generosity; the one who leads, with zeal; the one who does acts of mercy, with cheerfulness.

1 Corinthians 12:28–30—And God has appointed in the church first apostles, second prophets, third teachers, then miracles, then gifts of healing, helping, administrating, and various kinds of tongues. Are all apostles? Are all prophets? Are all teachers? Do all work miracles? Do all possess gifts of healing? Do all speak with tongues? Do all interpret?

James 1:5—If any of you lacks wisdom, let him ask of God, who gives to all liberally and without reproach, and it will be given to him.

Chapter Five

THE BELIEF AND PURPOSE OF PROPHECIES

Before proceeding, I ask that you take a few moments to contemplate these questions:

First, with regard to discerning and prophesying future events, do you believe in their existence? Second, how do you perceive they are revealed or given to people? After you have meditated and believe you have determined a response to these questions, then continue.

Now, the purpose for placing the following verses within this chapter is to prove biblically that God Himself says that He does nothing until He reveals the hidden things to His chosen servants, revealing them in visions and in dreams. I write this statement simply because many have neither understood nor fully accepted the fact, but have denied what God reveals in these sorts of ways. However, it is proved by the verses below and throughout the whole Bible that God gives warnings of the future to His servants/prophets beforehand in the form of visions and in dreams in order for them to advise the people to turn from their ways. And in spite of the truth that all faithful believers are considered servants of God, it must be acknowledged that not all servants will be shown these present-day events, nor those "which must shortly take place" as stated in Revelation 1:1 and 22:6. Nevertheless, as you begin to read these chapters, I urge that you patiently read each verse accordingly, evaluating the dreams within the "Prophetic Revelations" section in chapter six, dedicating yourself to prayer and His word, whereby you may gain the knowledge, wisdom, and understanding of it all before making a final determination.

Numbers 12:6—Then after commanding them to listen carefully, He said: "I, the LORD, speak to prophets in visions and dreams.

Amos 3:7—Surely the Lord GOD does nothing, unless He reveals His secret to His servants the prophets.

2 Peter 3:2—What God's prophets said would happen. You must never forget what the holy prophets taught in the past. And you must remember what the apostles told you our Lord and Savior has commanded us to do.

Revelation 22:6 Then he said to me, "These words are faithful and true." And the Lord God of the holy prophets sent His angel TO SHOW HIS SERVANTS THE THINGS WHICH MUST SHORTLY TAKE PLACE.

Chapter Six

PROPHETIC REVELATIONS

As we look into the events of our present time, it is troubling to witness the strange and unsettling events taking place throughout the world. These events, which are described throughout this book, have undoubtedly been taking place more often since the turn of the century. As I then began to compare the strangeness of these events with that of my dreams, I came to realize that the contents of these and other revelations that I had received throughout the past years were not of the normal pattern of dreams. Although I have received many types of these unusual dreams, know that of the few I describe in this book, some will seem closely related to one another, but the majority will bring out the importance of their own message: preparing for a worldwide economic disaster and a worldwide famine. Nevertheless, my purpose in writing this section is to provide the reader with the insight that what has been revealed to me is without a doubt gradually occurring throughout the world. Also read chapter eleven, for it describes other peculiar dreams that were shown to me relating to the church, its Leaders, and the people.

1.   In the months before the turn of the century, I recall seeing myself standing among many people and businesses. All of a sudden, as they looked up toward the sky, people began to scream. As they ran, I was supernaturally removed from their midst and placed on the side, along with a few others. When I looked up toward the sky, I noticed a huge black bull descending toward the earth. It went past me and the others in my group without touching or harming us, but

began to trample the businesses and the rest of the people who, unlike me, had not been taken to safety. When I woke up, I became somewhat concerned by the content of this dream because of my inability to fully comprehend its meaning. But as I began to share it with someone, they informed me that a similar bull was located in New York's Wall Street stock exchange area. I was then able to understand its meaning. It is a strange coincidence that what I have received seems to symbolize what is taking place throughout our nation: our stock market keeps fluctuating while the prices on items we buy are rising to an unaffordable level. At the same time, many businesses are struggling and downsizing while others are closing at an ever-increasing rate. Despite the fact that these things may seem more evident now than ever before, I believe this revelation pertains less to what is taking place at the present time than to what is to come: an economic collapse, as seen in the symbolic arrival of the black horse. "When He opened the third seal, I heard the third living creature say, 'Come and see.' So I looked, and behold, a black horse, and he who sat on it had a pair of scales in his hand. And I heard a voice in the midst of the four living creatures saying, 'A quart of wheat for a denarius (a day's wage)], and three quarts of barley for a denarius'" (Revelation 6:5-6).

Be forewarned, as soon as New York's economic market comes to its ultimate demise, the United States, together with the rest of the world, will without a doubt come into a Great Depression worse than the one that took place in 1929. This economic collapse, according to biblical description and prophecy, will bring about another major event unequal to any other (read Chapter 12 of The Return, the Truth: A Biblical and Spiritual Perspective). But how unfortunate that many have disregarded the warnings, failing to acknowledge that the deficits, overspending, and corruption taking place throughout many local, city, state, and federal agencies, as well as the lack of employment and higher prices, will also be among the causes that will eventually lead to the economic downfall and other events. Be assured, problems are coming, and they're going to get worse!

2. In this dream a powerful earthquake began to occur in New York City. As many rocks fell from everywhere, I looked around and saw a large pillar of rocks with someone sleeping on top of it, while another person was not noticing the earthquake that was taking place. So I asked him, "Can't you see what is happening?" He didn't respond. Then I looked out my window and was surprised to see a very large arm, covered in a hanging robe-type sleeve, with lightning and thunder coming out of its fingertip. I asked myself, "Could this be God's wrath or coming judgment, since it is evident that the people are spiritually asleep, becoming more ungodly than ever before, and not caring about their surroundings or godly matters— desiring to do as they please rather than wake up and turn from their sins? For what reason was such a thing revealed to me?" The answer might be found in the following verse: If my people who are called by My name humble themselves, and pray and seek My face and turn from their wicked ways, then I will hear from heaven and will forgive their sin and heal their land (2 Chronicles 7:14) .

3. One day as I was about to enter a church, I noticed that it was full. After I had waited outside for some time, the crowd gathered around the entrance allowed me to enter. As I was walking down the aisle, the preacher began to pray for me. When he finished, I noticed that I was standing in front of the podium (pulpit) overlooking the many people who were attending the service. Suddenly, I heard a voice that said to me, "Write the ten plagues of the Bible on ten pieces of paper." Two men came and began to assist me in writing the plagues, placing the papers in the offering plate. After the plagues were written, the voice, which I had known to be the Spirit of God, spoke to me again and said, "Now have nine people select nine out of the ten papers." But when I began to inform the people what the Spirit of God was instructing me to do, many began to leave because of their unbelief, and the church was left half empty. Now, as the offering plate was being passed, nine people randomly selected the papers as they had been instructed. The two men returned and handed me the offering plate. As I brought the

remaining paper to eye level, the Spirit of God said to me, "This is the last plague I am going to send down to the earth." Again, when I shared this message with the people, many more began to leave because of their lack of belief. As I turned toward the ministers, they laughed and rejected me, saying, "God would not do or say such things." However, this dream could not be more true, for as soon as I began to share this message with the people, many refused to believe. I was amazed by their lack of acceptance. Many of these people claimed to believe in God and His word, but undoubtedly lacked spiritual knowledge and biblical understanding. This brings to mind the story of Noah, in which the people refused to believe the message until judgment came, and by then it was too late. In prayer I asked God for a confirmation, and after a few days I received Revelation 3:10, which says, "Because you have kept My command to persevere, I also will keep you from the hour of trial which shall come upon the whole world, to test those who dwell on the earth. For further study of the ten plagues of the Bible, read Exodus, chapters 8 through 12.

4. This dream may seem to represent the events of September 11, 2001. However, because I found its contents reflecting present and future times, I decided to describe it here as well. During the early months of 2001, I dreamed that God, by calling out His name, had given me the ability to protect and rescue people who were in need and in danger. As I went about assisting those who were in need, I began to hear screams from New York City. When I arrived there, I began to see many people who were burning inside a large building; they were screaming, pleading for help. But as I called out the name of God in an attempt to enter the building to rescue them, I discovered that my ability was gone. Looking at the suffering of these people and feeling helpless, I became deeply emotional. As I stood there with tears in my eyes, a voice spoke to me from heaven and said, "You cannot save them for they are not calling out to My name."

5. I dreamed that I saw myself, one clear afternoon, looking over New York City from across the river. As I began to pray with my eyes lifted toward the sky, I noticed that the clouds began to move and join together, creating an opening in their center. While watching this strange sight, I noticed a dark cloud come out of this opening, make a sharp turn, and hover over the city. While it hovered there, I pointed to New York from across the river and said, "God is going to punish you for what you're doing." Could there be a reason why I was looking over New York City and noticing the water between us? Note: Sometime during the early months of 2006, I learned of a book written by a well-known minister at a New York City church; he described a vision of a similar cloud that hovered over the city. Mere coincidence? But know that on a few other occasions I had dreamed of tsunamis and floods that were coming toward New York.

6. In this dream from several years ago, I began to pray in the streets of New York City. Suddenly, as I lifted my head toward the sky, I noticed a large humanlike image, and as I gazed at this strange sight, I became aware that thunder and lightning were surrounding Him. After a brief moment, He spoke to me; "I am coming down to punish the earth for what it is doing." Then as I began to listen to the Book of Isaiah, I was surprised to hear that these words were spoken by Him as well. But could we discount these present-day worldwide disasters and weather patterns as natural in origin? Haven't we been witnessing more strange happenings than usual? "For behold, the LORD comes out of His place To punish the inhabitants of the earth for their iniquity" (Isaiah 26:21). "And there will be signs in the sun, in the moon, and in the stars; and on the earth distress of nations, with perplexity, the sea and the waves roaring; men's hearts failing them from fear and the expectation of those things which are coming on the earth, for the powers of the heavens will be shaken" (Luke 21:25 and 26).

7. A week after receiving the above, I again dreamed that I was taken from among the people and placed in a building along with a few others. When I looked around, I noticed two doors and a large window, and as I looked through the window, I was able to see a huge white hovering sphere. After a few moments, He spoke to me and said, "I am going to punish the earth for what it is doing." Immediately after that, He departed. After He returned, the two doors opened automatically, and those inside the building gathered and began to march in a group, praising God because we were finally going to meet Him. Then, as we began to go through New York City, I noticed that it was under construction. Read Revelation 3:10-3:11 and Revelation 18.

8. One afternoon as I was resting at my home, I heard a voice saying, "Many will be punished," but when I looked around, I wasn't able to find anyone. A month after receiving the above, I again was shown a major disaster that is to occur. And although calamities are occurring throughout the world, I believe the majority of this revelation does not pertain exclusively to what is now taking place in the world, but also to the disasters that are soon to come. Look at the previous two verses from Colossians 3 and the others as well. However, in July 2006, I again was given a message to advise the people that many events are about to happen.

9. In this dream, as I was taken up to heaven, I heard a voice that said, "He who was not found in the Book of Life will be thrown into the lake of fire." Then, as I looked toward the earth and marveled at it, I noticed three or four books being thrown down toward the earth by someone in heaven. When the books reached the earth's atmosphere, I said to myself, "They're not burning up." But after the books were thrown, I began to descend toward the earth without burning up either. As I finally reached the earth, someone came to me and said, "Follow me, I would like to show you something." When we arrived at a certain place, he pointed downward, and as I looked, I noticed that it was the lake of fire. But

19

as I looked further, I was able to see people who were burning in it. The books that were cast down represent judgments that will come upon the earth. And this is becoming evident from the events that have been taking place throughout the world. I am certain that most of us know what the lake of fire is and who will be going there. Revelation 21:8 states, "But the cowardly, unbelieving, abominable, murderers, sexually immoral, sorcerers, idolaters, and all liars shall have their part in the lake which burns with fire and brimstone, which is the second death." A month after I received the above, I was given a similar dream in which I saw myself descending toward the earth. While descending, I noticed a large body of water, but then I heard a voice that said, "The people will be accountable for their own sins."

10. In this short but disturbing revelation, I witnessed a famine taking place in New York City. All of a sudden, people desperately began looking for food. They searched frantically and chaotically, in supermarkets, garbage cans, and every other place, for whatever they could find, but because what had taken place was so severe, they were not able to find any food. Can we honestly believe we will elude this type of event and disaster? Have the people of America and the world forgotten the Great Depression of 1929? Are we not noticing the continued instability of our nation's economy and our rising prices?

11. One evening I dreamed that I was overlooking the ocean. Suddenly, an event took place that caused chaos. Again, people frantically searched for food, eventually turning against one another, stealing whatever they were able to find. But since food couldn't be found, they began to take live birds and hamsters from their cages in order to eat them. As these things took place, a voice spoke to me from heaven: "This is happening because I am angry at the people for the sins they are committing." Then as I looked throughout the surrounding buildings, I noticed the tenants standing on their terraces and looking toward the ocean in awe because of what was taking place. Could this be the foretelling of a tsunami followed by a

famine? Let it be known that many have had visions and dreams of this sort; unfortunately, their advice and warnings have gone unheard. Nevertheless, be advised that, on a couple of other occasions, what was also made known to me was God's anger toward the world because of the many sins people have been committing.

12. Between November 2006 and May 2007, I heard a voice that said, "I am going to search for the evil that all people—men, women, and prophets— are doing." After a couple of months had passed, He again spoke to me and said, "I am going to punish My servants who are not doing My will." A month later, as I was shown people within the church, He said, "I am going to punish the disobedient." After saying this, He turned and asked me, "Did you tell them what I told you to speak?"

13. In August 2007, I saw myself standing near the ocean. All of a sudden, as I turned to leave, a church of magnificent beauty began to rise from the depths of the water. As I stood gazing at the front of this church, I noticed an image of a person with her hands lifted toward the sky while praying to God. But then I noticed another image, which seemed to resemble Jesus Christ. His back was turned toward this person, and He had one hand covering one ear while the other hand was extended. As I continued gazing at this amazing sight, God began to give me the interpretation of this vision. After gaining the knowledge of its meaning, I became deeply emotional and began to advise people to turn from their sins, for God is no longer accepting or listening to their praises. But as many people ignored the message, a huge tidal wave began to form. Several individuals who heeded my warnings ran with me inside a building and were protected from the coming disaster. When I went around to see the damage the wave had caused, I was able to see that not much had taken place, only that the people continued to lie sleeping on the sand. As I looked at them, God informed me that this was just a warning for them to turn from their sins. The church and the

individual who had come up from the water represent a multitude of churches and people (see Revelation 17:15).

Isaiah 1:15-16: When you spread out your hands, I will hide My eyes from you; Even though you make many prayers, I will not hear. Your hands are full of blood. Wash yourselves, make yourselves clean; Put away the evil of your doings from before My eyes. Cease to do evil.

Proverbs 1:25–28: Because you disdained all my counsel, And would have none of my rebuke, I also will laugh at your calamity; I will mock when your terror comes, When your terror comes like a storm, And your destruction comes like a whirlwind, When distress and anguish come upon you. Then they will call on me, but I will not answer; They will seek me diligently, but they will not find me.

14. One evening as I slept, I began to dream of people who were prostrated with their hands extended outward, worshipping other gods. Then, as I stood troubled by what I had witnessed, a message was given to me advising me to read the Old Testament book of Zephaniah. As I listened to its passages, I became somewhat astounded, not only by its contents, but also by its revelation: Zephaniah's prophetic message of God's wrath was consistent with the dreams that I have received. My inability to remember this particular book of the Bible or ever having listened to its contents, is what continues to strike me about this extraordinary dream. (Read the book of Zephaniah, chapters 1 through 3.)

15. One evening, I dreamed that someone had taken me from the earth in order to view it from afar. At first, I noticed nothing unusual about the earth's appearance as it rotated in its normal clockwise motion. But, to my surprise, as I looked toward the upper left side, a very large arm with its finger pointing directly toward the earth had become visible. As I turned toward the earth again, I noticed that it began to slowly rotate in a counterclockwise manner.

And as I contemplated the strangeness of it all, the earth began to go up in flames. Read 2 Peter 3:7.

16. In this most peculiar dream, I noticed a withered tree with yellow leaves that had been cut down and placed in the living room of my home. Suddenly, out of nowhere, an owl flew past me and came to rest upon the lower part of the tree. As it stood there staring in my direction, I changed focus and turned toward the far left side of the room. Then, as I took notice of a bookshelf and contemplated the many books it contained, a voice spoke to me from within them and said, "I am going to punish the inhabitants of the earth." The withered tree perhaps symbolizes a season, while books, as stated in a previous dream, represent judgments that are to come.

The majority of these dreams seem to be directed toward New York. However, let it be known that on a few other occasions I was shown similar events that will take place throughout several other locations as well. In some of these dreams I have seen storms before they took place, earthquakes and tsunamis coming not only to New York but also to other places, a nuclear disaster in New York, terrorists seeking to attack the subway system before the events were shown on the news, and other countries banding together with terrorists looking for an open door in order to attack our nation. So if these things are part of normal subconscious dreaming, then why be concerned?

Are we prepared? Are we guaranteed this day or the day after tomorrow? You can be certain that according to my experience, many of the events revealed in the dreams that contain prophetic significance don't actually occur until months or years later. But given the uncertainty of these days, we can never be too sure of the timing, can we? Read Leviticus 26:14–44, where it states what God will do if and when His people continue to sin and turn from His ways. And as you read the verses, keep in mind that they were not intended for the Israelite nation alone, but for all of us who are considered God's people, and are not exempt either from any blessing or Judgment.

What, then, can be determined from the above? A tsunami? An earthquake? A nuclear attack? Or possibly all these disasters? Whatever situation New York City will face, you can be certain that any of these disasters can and will lead to an economic collapse followed by a famine and unfortunately many deaths (as I have seen in my dreams). But when I share this message with people, a few agree that something is bound to happen, while many others state that God will protect them so there's no need to prepare. Others are not certain but are not concerned. Overall, the majority of the people do not care, believing that if these things are bound to happen, then they will happen many years from now. However, if we acknowledge the disasters taking place throughout our time, what guarantees this nation is exempt? May I add, regarding these places that were revealed to me and to a few others, haven't we noticed a body of water surrounding them in one way or another? Do you prefer to be a live, foolish-looking believer like Noah in Genesis 6, or a mocking, unbelieving, dead duck like the people he had spoken to before the flood, who did not know the uncertainty of their future? Or are you wise enough to prepare beforehand? Are you certain you're prepared? Your choice! Read Revelation 3:10.

Our fluctuating economy, which is presently one of our main concerns and is spoken of daily by the media, has moved to a level of troubling instability. Today, the Great Depression of 1929—the Crash—is a painful memory for those who survived it. In essence, we should take into account the events of that day, which serve both as a matter of historical interest and as a warning of future pain and suffering. For it was once established that our government was to never get involved or interfere with the free enterprise economic system. This advice, as well as the warnings of an impending judgment, which many have prophesied throughout the years, has not only been ignored but is also presently being dismissed. The borrowing, overspending, and inflation of our economy by the government may cause us to enter into an economic dilemma. We may blame the leaders of America, but if we, the nations of this world, examine our morals and spiritual values and accept self-blame for this unprecedented predicament, we will comprehend that its cause is not primarily our government's incompetent decisions, but our own ungodly choices. Therefore, unless an appropriate level of godliness becomes evident throughout the churches, America, and the nations of the world, be assured that any efforts to stabilize the economic crisis will unfortunately result in failure.

Accordingly, with regard to the fluctuation and instability of our nation's financial system, could it be that we are once again on the verge of another Great Depression?

Will hyperinflation (the printing of additional currency) reduce the value of our nation's dollar to a worthless penny? Have you compared the value of our dollar with that of the euro? Would the crippling of our economy bring the world's greatest power to the status of a poverty-stricken nation? Will our bank accounts be insured by the federal government? Will government aid be unavailable, due to the severity of an economic calamity? Will law enforcement have control over mass riots?

Although several have considered the contents of this book and the interpretation of these dreams to be a matter of opinion, if what I provide here was written under false pretenses, never to happen, then you will lose nothing. But if what is being presented came about from the truth by godly discernment, and is rejected, then as a consequence, you will definitely lose everything. Even if certain individuals are skeptical about these revelations, can they honestly deny the facts that relate the revelation of the black bull with the instability of our nation's economy?

<u>The following passages will give people an insight into the consequences coming upon those bringing deception by the prophecy of false visions, dreams, and messages not spoken or revealed by God.</u>

Ezekiel 13:3—Thus says the Lord GOD: "Woe to the foolish prophets, who follow their own spirit and have seen nothing!"

Ezekiel 13:7-9—Have you not seen a futile vision, and have you not spoken false divination? You say, "The LORD says," but I have not spoken. Therefore thus says the Lord GOD: "Because you have spoken nonsense and envisioned lies, therefore I am indeed against you," says the Lord GOD. "My hand will be against the prophets who envision futility and who divine lies."

Jeremiah 14:15—Therefore thus says the LORD concerning the prophets who prophesy in My name, whom I did not send, and who say, "Sword and famine shall not be in this land"—By sword and famine those prophets shall be consumed!

Jeremiah 23:25-26—I have heard what the prophets have said who prophesy lies in My name, saying, "I have dreamed, I have dreamed!" How long will this be in the heart of the prophets who prophesy lies? Indeed they are prophets of the deceit of their own heart,

Jeremiah 23:28–32—"The prophet who has a dream, let him tell a dream; And he who has My word, let him speak My word faithfully. What is the chaff to the wheat?" says the LORD. "Is not My word like a fire?" says the LORD, "And like a hammer that breaks the rock in pieces? Therefore behold, I am against the prophets," says the LORD, "who steal My words every one from his neighbor. Behold, I am against the prophets," says the LORD, "who use their tongues and say, 'He says.' Behold, I am against those who prophesy false dreams," says the LORD, "and tell them, and cause My people to err by their lies and by their recklessness. Yet I did not send them or command them; therefore they shall not profit this people at all," says the LORD.

Deuteronomy 18:20–22—But the prophet who presumes to speak a word in My name, which I have not commanded him to speak, or who speaks in the name of other gods, that prophet shall die.' And if you say in your heart, 'How shall we know the word which the LORD has not spoken?' when a prophet speaks in the name of the LORD, if the thing does not happen or come to pass, that is the thing which the LORD has not spoken; the prophet has spoken it presumptuously; you shall not be afraid of him.

We must all come to understand that we are now living in a time of uncertainty. Our government, despite its deception, lies, corruption, and overspending, should not be held completely accountable for any disaster that will unfortunately be visited upon our nation. Again, Second Chronicles 7:14 states, "If My people who are called by My name will humble themselves, and pray and seek My face, and turn from their wicked ways, then I will hear from heaven, and will forgive their sin and heal their land." Also in Jeremiah 2:35, You say, "I am innocent; surely his anger has turned from me." Behold, I will bring you to judgment for saying, "'I have not sinned.

Jeremiah 25:29–32—For behold, I begin to work disaster at the city that is called by my name, and shall you go unpunished? You shall not go unpunished, for I am summoning a sword against all the inhabitants of the earth, declares the LORD of hosts.' "You, therefore, shall prophesy against them all these words, and say to them: "'The LORD will roar from on high, and from his holy habitation utter his voice; he will roar mightily against his fold, and shout, like those who tread grapes, against all the inhabitants of the earth. The clamor will resound to the ends of the earth, for the LORD has an indictment against the nations; he is entering into judgment with all flesh, and the wicked he will put to the sword, declares the LORD.' "Thus says the LORD of hosts: Behold, disaster is going forth from nation to nation, and a great tempest is stirring from the farthest parts of the earth!

Could the significance of these and other revelations that have been occurring throughout the world be that we are now at the commencement of the Final Judgment?

Proverbs 11:4—Riches do not profit in the day of wrath, but righteousness delivers from death.

Chapter Seven

New York in the Book of Revelation

The following paragraphs contain a brief description of possible evidence in the Bible regarding the events in New York City on September 11, 2001. Despite the fact that this was a day of terror, distress, and sorrow for many, it is of great importance that we value the memory of those who lost their lives on that day, giving special recognition and admiration to those who served and protected our people, city, and nation. We should also extend unceasing love and sympathy to all who lost a loved one, not neglecting their needs or forgetting the pain and suffering stemming from their loss. But as we continue in this effort, we should never forget that the word of God must be spoken and taught in its truth and never neglected regardless of past, present, or future circumstances.

As you read the passages in Revelation 18, you will notice that the writer, during his vision, seems to be describing New York City, or even America itself, as "Babylon the Great." For many years, it has been stated that New York is considered a great city, if not one of the greatest cities in the world. Yet it has a reputation as a present-day Sodom and Gomorrah, a city where abomination lies, a sinful place that has not turned from its wicked ways despite the many warnings about its impending Day of Judgment. Detestable sins have piled up to the skies: people have no fear of God but continue in idolatry, envy, greed, jealousy, pride in their luxuries, adultery, fornication, freedom of homosexuality, and the parading of such (Leviticus

20:13, Romans 1:26–27, and 1 Corinthians 6:9). Leaders make laws that are against God's people and detestable in His sight—laws that have changed our constitutional amendments and are against what our forefathers had originally established and instituted under God— eventually eliminating religion and prayer from our schools. They have no problem celebrating and allowing Halloween festivities rather than the Nativity, or preventing our children from pledging allegiance to our own U.S. flag or repeating any other pledge that includes the name of God, not acknowledging that removing the Ten Commandments from our U.S. courtrooms will not only harm our nation, but themselves as well.

America seems to be headed toward Communism, bringing about its own financial downfall, indiscriminately attacking the American way, and being blinded by evil itself. It does not recognize that its downfall is due to its own sins and incompetence, that breaking laws against discrimination and freedom of speech and religion is hypocritical. Rather than following those who act in such an ungodly way, a true American leader would be someone who would take a bold stand by upholding the name of God. How can the people in this unbelieving nation proclaim "In God We Trust" when they are attempting to eliminate His very name? What God does America believe in or serve? Could we honestly expect our nation to excel and be prosperous if what it has been doing is not in line with His ways? Matthew 6:24 states, "For you cannot serve both God and Money." God is distancing Himself from our land; His protection is evidently being removed from this nation. He will eventually bring His final judgment upon us. Our economy and land He will ravish, eventually giving us over into the hands of our enemies, for His anger toward this sinful world has not subsided. Neither will His wrath relent until people, especially the corrupt governments of America and the world, turn from their wicked ways. Then the abundance of God's riches will overflow through our land.

As you begin to read the following paragraph, notice the key verses from Revelation 18 that seem to describe certain events that took place on September 11, 2001. But as you closely study the verses within the chapter, you will come to realize that the sinful conditions and values described in these passages are closely related to the excess materialism found in New York City or America itself. A few years before the World Trade Center buildings collapsed, people said that New York City was a safe place to be. They boasted about her luxuries, stating that the Twin Tower buildings were extremely stable and would never be brought down. But as you may recall, at that very hour the plague of fire brought New York City down (Revelation 18:8), leaving one tower to become a "widow," since one fell before the other, which no longer had its companion. And when Revelation 18:7 states, "I sit as Queen," could it be describing New York City, the Twin Towers, the Statue of Liberty, or just another place? So I ask, pay close attention to the key details of the events within this chapter, for it will broaden your understanding of its relationship with the events of that day.

During the time of their destruction, the collapse of these towers unleashed a blast of harmful dust that up to this day has caused serious consequences, bringing a plague of sickness or eventually death to those who inhaled it. And although several individuals have believed that the beginning verses of this chapter signify the complete destruction of a city, as you turn to verse 21 you will be able to acknowledge that this assumption is incorrect, since the place of which this verse speaks seems to be facing its ultimate destruction at that very time.

1. As you read, ask yourself if the verses in the following passages from Revelation 18 could be describing the United States or New York City and the destruction of the World Trade Center buildings. Could verse 3 be referring to the stock market of New York City, since the kings and the merchants of the earth have participated not only in America's "power of her luxurious living," but also in New York City's riches? Is there any other place like America that has taken pride in her luxuries?

Revelation 18:3—For all nations have drunk the wine of the passion of her sexual immorality, and the kings of the earth have committed immorality with her, and the MERCHANTS of the earth HAVE GROWN RICH FROM THE POWER OF HER LUXURIOUS LIVING.

Revelation 18:7—As she glorified herself and lived in luxury, so give her a like measure of torment and mourning, since in her heart she says, "I sit as a queen, I am no widow, and mourning I shall never see."

2.   Several individuals have assumed that the verses below seem to describe a city that is being destroyed. However, if you relate these verses, along with verse 21, to the destruction of the World Trade Center, you will notice that this is a mistaken assumption because the destruction is not evident until verse 21. Yet, as you continue to read these passages, you will notice that certain verses describe a market of goods. Could these verses be describing the stock market of New York City? Or do they appear to be describing another place?

Revelation 18:8–13—For this reason her plagues will come in a single day, death and mourning and famine, and she will be burned up with fire; for mighty is the Lord God who has judged her. And the kings of the earth, who committed sexual immorality and lived in luxury with her, will weep and wail over her when they see the smoke of her burning. They will stand far off, in fear of her torment, and say, "Alas! Alas! You great city, you mighty city, Babylon! For in a single hour your judgment has come." And the merchants of the earth weep and mourn for her, since no one buys their cargo anymore, cargo of gold, silver, jewels, pearls, fine linen, purple cloth, silk, scarlet cloth, all kinds of scented wood, all kinds of articles of ivory, all kinds of articles of costly wood, bronze, iron and marble, cinnamon, spice, incense, myrrh, frankincense, wine, oil, fine flour, wheat, cattle and sheep, horses and chariots, and slaves, that is, human souls.

Revelation 18:15–19—The merchants of these wares, who gained wealth from her, will stand far off, in fear of her torment, weeping and mourning aloud, "Alas, alas, for the great city that was clothed in fine linen, in purple and scarlet, adorned with gold, with jewels, and with pearls! For in a single hour all this wealth has been laid waste." And all shipmasters and seafaring men, sailors and all whose trade is on the sea, stood far off and cried out as they saw the smoke of her burning, "What city was like the great city?" And they threw dust on their heads as they wept and mourned, crying out, "Alas, alas, for the great city where all who had ships at sea grew rich by her wealth! For in a single hour she has been laid waste."

3. Now, according to the above verses and the events that were revealed to me (see the "Prophetic Revelation" section in Chapter 6), could this be one of the unfortunate events that is to come upon New York City? Notice that when the mighty angel takes a "stone like a great millstone" and throws it into the sea, the city "will be found no more." Doesn't this appear to be describing destruction from a tsunami or a massive flood?

Revelation 18:21–23—Then a mighty angel took up a stone like a great millstone and threw it into the sea, saying, "So will Babylon the great city be thrown down with violence, and will be found no more; and the sound of harpists and musicians, of flute players and trumpeters, will be heard in you no more, and a craftsman of any craft will be found in you no more, and the sound of the mill will be heard in you no more, and the light of a lamp will shine in you no more, and the voice of bridegroom and bride will be heard in you no more, for your merchants were the great ones of the earth, and all nations were deceived by your sorcery."

Therefore, by this determination, could we conclude that the above passages from the second illustration are referring to the time of the city's destruction?

New York City and America, yes, you are what the Bible describes as "Babylon the Great." A "Great City" that will not be uprooted as it was, a beautiful city that has held many up because of their riches. All nations will mourn because of you, a mourning of darkness that, because of the abominations which are also being committed throughout the world, will cause many to be brought to their knees and to suffer.

Chapter Eight

Why New York City?

For several years the earth has been going through a series of unusual changes, causing catastrophic events throughout our world that many believe are due to what they call "global warming." But what these individuals refuse to acknowledge and accept is that these works are done by God Himself, working with our own natural environment. Being the "Beginning and the End," He is the Creator of rain, snow, hurricanes, tornadoes, tsunamis and such, some coming for the sole purpose of helping in our daily living, others as the consequences of our sins in order for us to repent of them. However, in either case, I urge that you begin to read the Bible and gain the understanding that God does make use of our own natural environment, or the things of "nature," in order to bring His punishments upon this sinful world, despite the fact His desire is to refrain from doing so.

But several have asked, "Why is New York City the target of a judgment or disaster if other nations are evidently worse than New York?"

Although there isn't a specific answer to this question, the primary reason is our own iniquities. We should also acknowledge that God Himself sees and knows all things, revealing to His servants certain (not all) hidden secrets that He alone knows (read Amos 3:7 and Revelation 22:6). But as you continue to read, I am certain that what God has revealed to me will help you gain a better understanding of the reasons for His judgment. And our focus shouldn't be on the question of His actions, but on the decisions that will keep us from wrong, and that will carry us through to salvation, since the decision of His judgments, or blessings, are His alone and are unmistakably justified. Nevertheless, as you continue to read these chapters, you will see that New York City will not be the only place that will come into judgment. This is becoming evident from the events that have been taking place throughout the world. Read 2 Peter 3:5–9.

Chapter Nine

Disasters from Our Past

Although it is a proven fact that God protects certain people in times of danger, it is imperative that individuals take responsibility for seeking God, praying, and maintaining themselves in a godly manner by reading His word on a daily basis. From this they can gain the knowledge, wisdom, and understanding of how He works when it comes to such things. But certain individuals believe that it is not of great importance to stock up on life's necessities if there is a warning of impending danger, since they believe that God will protect them from whatever may come. They quote but eventually misinterpret the biblical verse, "For God has not appointed us to suffer wrath, but to receive Salvation through our Lord Jesus Christ" (1 Thessalonians 5:9).

Haven't we seen, heard, or known about good churchgoing people who suffered in one way or another because they lacked what they needed to survive? In order to bring these people out of this erroneous belief, I have listed a few events that took place not only in biblical times but during the twentieth and twenty-first centuries as well.

1. In Genesis chapter 6, we see an interesting story about a man named Noah who was chosen by God to bring the message to the people of His imminent Day of Judgment. I am more than certain that Noah, among all the people that lived on the earth in those days, wasn't the only person who believed, sought, or prayed to God (just as we do in the present day). But since God acknowledged

the level of Noah's belief and obedience, He chose him to bring the message to the people of what was soon to come. Now, according to the Bible, did anyone believe or listen to the message God instructed Noah to speak? Apparently not, for if they did, they would have been with him in the ark, protected from the punishment as well. But what a shame that not even those who believed and prayed to God accepted Noah's message, because it evidently cost them their lives. And how disastrous that day must have been: the screams of thousands of people, many of them frantically pounding on the ark, pleading with Noah to save them from the disaster.

In so like manner, God is using a handful of people these days to speak on what will soon take place and what needs to be done in order for them to be protected. But just as in the time of Noah, not many people these days, including church-going people, believe either, saying, as I've heard others say: "If anything happens, God will protect me," clearly having a misconception about how God works when it comes to such things. But from among all the people of those days, wasn't Noah the only person whom God had chosen and spoken to about what was going to happen ...? And nobody listened. Didn't God also INSTRUCT Noah in chapter 6 of Genesis to STORE FOOD for him, his family, and the animals? So if this is the case, then how do people expect to obtain food and receive God's protection, if what they do is refuse to believe and not listen to His servants about what's coming? Haven't we learned from the past yet? Is God so unfair that He would bring judgment without prior warning? Aren't you noticing the frequent and unusual changes and disasters that have been taking place throughout the world? For God's Day of Judgment is eminent and is already at hand; will you be protected and prepared for that day? Amos 3:7 – Surely the Lord God does nothing, unless He reveals His secret to His servants the prophets.

2.   Another example is in the story of Joseph; you could begin to read it in Genesis chapter 39. How were he, his family, and the people of Egypt protected from the famine? Was it by God bringing

food down from heaven? No! God chose Joseph, an Israelite, who was sold into slavery by his own brothers, to fulfill His divine plan, using and preparing him to interpret Pharaoh's dream of a coming famine. In this way God protected Joseph, his family, and all of Egypt from hunger and death. But unlike Pharaoh, will the people of this age believe and accept dreams and their interpretations?

3. In Matthew 14, Mark 6 and 8, Luke 9, and John 6, we see another interesting story: of Jesus miraculously feeding a multitude of people with just a few loaves of bread and a couple of fish. However, if you notice, the food was not brought down from heaven, but was multiplied by Jesus in accordance with His power to perform miracles. In the same manner, when you read Acts 11:27–29, you will see that in the time of famine the disciples helped those who were in need, "each according to his ability." "His ability" in this case seems to signify the power of performing the same miracle as Jesus had performed when He fed the multitude. But unlike those days, do we earnestly ask and seek God in prayer and fasting to receive this type of spiritual gift? (Read 1 Corinthians 12:10.) So then, how will you be able to receive what is needed in order to survive when your desire is to refuse to believe, and to reject the messages that God has instructed His chosen servants to speak? Will the people be able to find food in a supermarket or will they prefer to look and eat from a trash bin, hoping to find something there? Haven't you read what Luke 10:16 states: "He who hears you hears Me, he who rejects you rejects Me, and he who rejects Me rejects Him who sent Me." Also, in Matthew 12:30: "He Who is not with Me is against Me, and he who does not gather with Me scatters abroad."

4. Now I will give a brief description on what took place in New York City seventy-seven years ago.

As many remember, it was an early Tuesday morning on October 29, 1929, since known as "Black Tuesday." As the stock market opened, the traders went about doing business, not suspecting what was to take place on that day. Suddenly, the market crashed, bringing an immediate frenzy of chaos, suicides, bankruptcy, unemployment, poverty, hunger, destruction of families, etc., throughout the United States and other parts of the world, traumatically changing the lives of many: a depression has just begun (do research on the Great Depression of 1929). But I would like to ask several important questions: First, how many people, or even God's messengers, warned about that coming day? Second, how many believed, listened, and were protected because they took action beforehand? Third, how many people searched for food in the streets and in garbage cans in order to survive? Fourth, what prevents this from happening again? Nothing! For the people of all nations and religious denominations have become more sinful than ever before, and are provoking God into His judgment. So I urge you: repent from any wrongful, sinful ways, read your Bible, and submit yourselves therefore to God; resist evil and it will depart from you.

5. This is an important example we should live by, believing and accepting that disasters do occur anywhere and at any time. And although the people did receive forewarnings, know however that other places were not as fortunate, since the disaster that these places had received came upon them at an unsuspected time. In 2005 Hurricane Katrina came to the United States, overcoming the New Orleans area of Louisiana, destroying the city, causing deaths and much suffering to many people. But just as asked earlier, how many messengers did God use in order to protect those before Katrina hit? And how many people who lived there were of a church and unfortunately suffered or lost their lives because they refused to listen to the warnings? So then, how can the people be protected if what they do is reject the messengers God has been sending? Has anyone received any other message than the one written here? Did God speak to anyone, saying not to worry, they can go about their ways as they please without any consequences, He will bring food down from heaven to protect them? If so, then why didn't it happen during hurricane Katrina and all the many other disasters that have taken

place throughout the world? Has God been wasting His time using prophets and messengers to advise us? Is God unjust? No! But we are.

Now I strongly urge that you pay close attention to what is taking place throughout the world and acknowledge the messengers who have been stating, "God warns us to prepare for what is to come," just as He revealed to Noah, Joseph, Isaiah, and the many others who have warned of a coming judgment.

Proverbs 22:3—The prudent sees danger and hides himself, but the simple go on and suffer for it.

Chapter Ten

The Misleading Fact

For several years I have come across many individuals who believe that God is not a God of judgment or of punishments. Stating that those consequences will not come upon us because He is a holy God of love and compassion, they believe that such things come either from the evil one (Satan) or human error itself. Such statements are foolish and not necessarily true, for one of the major reasons we have been witnessing disasters and changes throughout the earth is undoubtedly the many sins being committed without recognition or repentance. While God did not abandon us, we have abandoned Him and the good He wants us to practice. God loves His people and His creation, but we must admit that we have taken advantage of His love, mercy, and patience. If we closely read the Bible, we will see that He is in command of all things, disciplining us and sending punishments because of His love toward us, desiring that we refrain from the constant sins that He detests (Colossians 3:5–6, Hebrews 12:29).

But do not be misled into believing that it is permissible to do as we please without any consequences (1 John 2:15–17), that judgments are not for us because we no longer live by the laws of the Old Testament but are living under grace. I urge you, do not be misled or fall into these false assumptions and foolish teachings. For as it states in Romans 6:15, "What then? Are we to sin because we are not under law but under grace? By no means." So understand that the purpose God sent His son into the world was for the world to be saved through Him by the shedding of His blood on the cross once for our sins, and not for us to deliberately continue in them and so bring Him back to His crucifixion. For Jesus said in Matthew 5:17, "Do not think that I have come to abolish the Law or the Prophets, I have not come to abolish them but to fulfill them." He also says in Matthew 5:18, "For truly, I say to you, until heaven and earth pass away, not an Iota, not a dot, will pass from the Law until all is accomplished." Also read Ezekiel 7, Jeremiah 2:35, Jeremiah 25:29-32, and Revelation 16:1.

Therefore, if you read the laws of the Old Testament, I am certain that you will be able to see that several of our present-day laws and prophecies seem to have originated from them as well. So if you're one to believe that God is not involved in the affairs of the earth because of the Old to the New Testament transition, then let it be known that you are greatly mistaken, since it states in 1 Corinthians 11:3, "But I want you to understand that the head of every man is Christ, the head of a wife is her husband, and the head of Christ is God." So you see, God, no matter what, is still the Head of all things. Therefore read your Bible and gain the understanding of how God works when it comes to such things, acknowledging that He is a God of much love, mercy, and patience, but also of discipline and punishments..

Malachi 3:6—For I am the LORD, I do not change.

Jeremiah 18:7–10—The instant I speak concerning a nation and concerning a kingdom, to pluck up, to pull down, and to destroy it, if that nation against whom I have spoken turns from its evil, I will relent of the disaster that I thought to bring upon it. And the instant I speak concerning a nation and concerning a kingdom, to build and to plant it, if it does evil in My sight so that it does not obey My voice, then I will relent concerning the good with which I said I would benefit it. And again, read 2 Chronicles 7:14.

A Comparative Insight

The higher authorities of this world have established certain laws from within their place of governing. If these laws are not obeyed, judgment and punishment follow. In like manner, God, for thousands of years, has established His laws that should be obeyed, and ignoring, overlooking, or disregarding them in any way will cause you to be subjected to judgment as well. Therefore, do not believe that our ways are God's ways or the ways of righteousness, for it states in Proverbs 16:25, "There is a way that seems right to a man, but its end is the way to death." And Matthew 10:28 tells us, "Do not be afraid of those who kill the body but cannot kill the soul; rather be afraid of the One who could destroy both soul and body in Hell."

The Attachment of One

Sin has been in existence since the beginning of time. However, what some don't realize or refuse to acknowledge is that each sin gives birth to another and multiplies into several additional sins that are worse than the original. This happens without one even acknowledging its expansion. Jealousy, hatred, greed, adultery, fornication, stealing, etc. could branch out and develop into other sins. For example, greed can force a person to embezzle thousands if not millions of dollars from their corporation. This corruption can cause other companies to go into decline, forcing them to file for bankruptcy or even go out of business. This would bring layoffs and much frustration to many, including families that are unable to keep their homes, eventually causing higher prices on certain things that the consumer must bear and bringing our stock market to fluctuate at an unstable level. Not only does this fall under the sin of greed but also of stealing, lying, deception, coveting, malicious intent, etc. This is just one example of how a sin can expand and multiply.

Another actual example that occurs each and every day is the sin of lying. It can also fall under the category of greed, but I will use it within a separate context in order to give the meaning of its purpose. As we know, lying takes place each day, even within our churches. But as we have seen, lying can consist of false claims as well as accusations against others in order to make a fast buck. Some examples include filing false claims with government agencies in order to receive financial assistance, or even suing insurance companies, claiming to have received an injury from a car accident or in the workplace. As I stated above, these do not fall only under the sin of lying but of greed, stealing, etc. For money can with time lead a person into the temptation to commit other immoralities in order to satisfy his or her desires. And how unfortunate that certain individuals from within the church are in commitment to these things, believing that they are not causing harm to anyone. How mistaken they are to believe such foolishness.

In a similar manner, adultery also branches into other sins like fornication, deception, coveting, lying, stealing, and envy. So is it clear how one wrongdoing can develop into many? Therefore, if a person claims that he or she only did one wrong, they must evaluate themselves to determine whether or not the sin had multiplied into three, five, or even eight. But please do not attempt to quote the commandment "Love thy neighbor as thyself" in order to justify this sin.

The Unknowledgeable Judges

Although the material below may not directly RELATE to what is written in these chapters, be informed that the purpose for placing it in this section is to educate people, especially the church, as well as to provide biblical knowledge of the truth as it relates to the teachings of these events.

On numerous occasions, several individuals have asked, "What will be the destination of those who have suffered much in this world but never had the opportunity to repent of their wrongs before passing on?" Although the depth of this question has caused much curiosity, in order to avoid potential for false judgment, I decided to remain neutral and researched this question further. As I began to listen to the Bible, I came across several passages that seem to bring the main question better into perspective. Nevertheless, the purpose for writing this paragraph was to give certain individuals the insight that suffering alone, without repentance, is not the key to salvation. And I myself, according to my experiences, am able to testify to this.

Luke 13:2–5—And He answered them, "Do you think that these Galileans were worse sinners than all the other Galileans, because they suffered in this way? No, I tell you; but unless you repent, you will all likewise perish. Or those eighteen on whom the tower in Siloam fell and killed them: do you think that they were worse offenders than all the others who lived in Jerusalem? No, I tell you; but unless you repent, you will all likewise perish."

2 Corinthians 7:9-10—As it is, I rejoice, not because you were grieved, but because you were grieved into repenting. For you felt a godly grief, so that you suffered no loss through us. For godly grief produces a repentance that leads to salvation without regret, whereas worldly grief produces death.

One evening, as I further meditated on this question, I began to dwell on several verses from Revelation 20. As I listened to these passages, I began to question several teachings and religious beliefs. As you read verse 13 of this chapter, ask yourself: during the Day of Judgment, why are the souls of people being brought out of three places (sea, Death, and Hades) and not directly from hell, as many have stated, when it is believed that they have passed on without salvation?

Revelation 20:12–15—And I saw the dead, small and great, standing before God, and books were opened. And another book was opened, which is the Book of Life. And the dead were judged according to their works, by the things which were written in the books. The sea gave up the dead who were in it, and Death and Hades delivered up the dead who were in them. And they were judged, each one according to his works. Then Death and Hades were cast into the lake of fire. This is the second death. And anyone not found written in the Book of Life was cast into the lake of fire.

As I reflected on the mystery and curiousness of the above passages, another question came to mind. If it's been stated that the souls of those who didn't have the opportunity to accept the Word were not saved, but went to hell (Hades) despite their belief in Christ and their good works, then, when the Books and the Book of Life are opened, why will some be found in the Book of Life and not others? Does it make sense for people to be sent to Hell, and then find them written in the Book of Life because they were found worthy due to their good works?

As I meditated and brought these things into prayer, I came to the conclusion that these verses are referring not to the time that many have called "the rapture," but to its aftermath. When you read the contents of Revelation 20, referencing it with the above-stated passages (Revelation 20:12–15), this becomes clear. For if these passages were indeed referring to the rapture, as some believe, there wouldn't be any purpose in being removed from the earth at that time in order to determine if one will be found worthy to enter into His kingdom. Isn't this the reason one will be taken up (raptured) beforehand? Nevertheless, though a person may not enter into heaven after their death due to their lack of acceptance and/or repentance as evident throughout the Bible, because of their beliefs in Christ (John 3:18, 1 John 5:13) and "according to his works" (Revelation 20:13), they are found worthy at that time to enter into heaven and not hell or the lake of fire.

Although these questions and statements are just my interpretation of these verses, it is of utmost importance for all people to recognize and repent of their sins (Acts 3:19), not judging in any unbiblical and needless manner (Matthew 7:1 and 2, Luke

6:37, and John 7:24), but accepting the ways and commands of God, in order to escape that judgment and obtain the opportunity to enter into heaven (read Luke 13:2–5 and 2 Corinthians 7:9 and 10) . For according to the evidence of these passages, despite your good works, not many names will be found written in the Book of Life. As Hebrews 12:14 states, "Pursue peace with all people, and holiness, without which no one will see the Lord." Also read Matthew 19:16-21.

James 1:21—Therefore lay aside all filthiness and overflow of wickedness, and receive with meekness the implanted word, which is able to save your souls.

The Controversy of the Adorned Temple

For several years, the church, for various reasons, has gone through issues that resulted in the loss of members and attendance. Although these issues vary, one area that I have found to be somewhat of a concern is the criticism of the focus on the outward appearance of others. Despite my skepticism about the intrusion of church doctrine, I cite several biblical passages in order to help the church and others obtain an insight into the truth about this controversy and gain some understanding of it.

Now, If we turn to the Bible for guidance, we will be able to comprehend that God is not One to look upon the outward appearance of a person, but at the purity of one's heart, clearly giving us an indication that loss of spirituality does not come so much from one's physical appearance, but from the sinful desire of the heart. As 1 Samuel 16:7 says, "For the LORD does not see as man sees; for man looks at the outward appearance, but the LORD looks at the heart." And 1 Peter 3:3–4 states, "Do not let your adornment be merely outward arranging the hair, wearing gold, or putting on fine apparel. Rather let it be the hidden person of the heart, with the incorruptible beauty of a gentle and quiet spirit, which is very precious in the sight of God."

This biblical passage should not be misinterpreted as asking people to refrain from wearing outward adornment. It advises us that however beautifully a person may present themselves outwardly, their heart should be in an even more beautiful state of purity, humbleness, and obedience (notice the word "merely"). Therefore, according to the Bible, I am certain that we are able to conclude that God is not concerned by petty issues such as who is or isn't cutting their hair, nor by the slightest dab of makeup a woman desires to put on her face, for God has no objection to His people looking their best in an appropriate but presentable manner. And although several doctrines differ, which would you honestly believe God prefers—a lost soul, or one who is outwardly and appropriately presentable? Do you not believe that hypocrisy and criticism are more of a sin than is wearing this or not wearing that? Isn't the purity of a person's heart of greater value than the outward appearance? For it states in Matthew 23:28, "Even so you also outwardly appear righteous to men, but inside you are full of hypocrisy and lawlessness." And in John 7:24 it says, "Do not judge according to appearance, but judge with righteous judgment." Also read Matthew 23:25–27 and 1 Peter 3:5.

Therefore, keep in mind that God, according to the Bible, is not concerned with or focused on the garment a man or woman wears, but with how it is being worn, what is being revealed, and the purpose for wearing it. For as Deuteronomy 22:5 states, "A woman shall not wear a man's garment, nor shall a man put on a woman's cloak, for whoever does these things is an abomination to the Lord your God." Can you discern the true meaning of this verse? Do you believe it is appropriate for a man to wear a feminine outfit? Or for a woman to wear a man's attire? Would you attempt to provoke God by doing such foolishness? Are you able to acknowledge that this is the abomination that God detests? If you see the garments that were worn in days of old, you will be able to determine that they were designed with different styles, patterns, colors, and shapes specifically made for each gender, in the same manner of design that is made for the people of this present day.

The church of God should recognize itself and avoid its criticism and hypocrisy, for a man has a physical body that a woman desires and a woman has a physical body that a man desires. So is there a difference regarding who gets tempted? Aren't we all tempted? If we come to look at what the dress code of the church should be, let's all wear what was worn in the past; otherwise, hold to your judgments and recognize yourself and wear your clothing in accordance with the design that was made for that gender, wearing it in an appropriate, modest, respectful, non-revealing, non-provocative manner. We must correct the wrong by the knowledge of His word and not from our own religious beliefs or self-judgments, for it states in Luke 6:37, "Judge not, and you shall not be judged. Condemn not, and you shall not be condemned. Forgive, and you will be forgiven." Therefore, we must recognize and evaluate ourselves in order to perceive if the plank we have in our eyes is less or greater than what the other person has in theirs. So read your Bible and obtain an understanding of the sins and disobediences that will keep us from entering into God's kingdom. Read Luke 6:41–42 and Revelation 21:8.

Chapter Eleven

The Church, Its Leaders, The People

As the months and years passed, I began to receive additional revelations pertaining to the condition of some church denominations and of their leaders. In these revelations I was shown leaders who were sleeping on a cross, on their altars, and on a floor of sand underneath their benches. Along with this I was able to see the lack of a foundation, and that there was garbage; black soil; dirty water; even feces on their altars, in addition to other filthy conditions within the church. The leaders who appeared in my dreams are the very same individuals who corrupt the church and destroy the remaining flock, not caring about who leaves or who desires to leave. They only desire to do as they please with everything and everyone, rejecting even those who come to speak in the name of the Lord and bring the Word in its truth. Hasn't it been acknowledged that whosoever does these things and rejects the truth, God will also reject? "'Woe to the shepherds who destroy and scatter the sheep of My pasture!' says the LORD. Therefore thus says the LORD God of Israel against the shepherds who feed His people: 'You have scattered My flock, driven them away, and not attended to them. Behold, I will attend to you for the evil of your doings'" (Jeremiah 23:1–2). Luke 10:16 states, "The one who hears you hears Me, and the one who rejects you rejects Me, and the one who rejects Me rejects Him who sent Me." And John 13:20 states, "Truly, truly, I say to you, whoever receives the one I send receives Me, and whoever receives Me receives the One who sent Me." Also read Jeremiah 25:34–37.

So I ask: How can people, especially church leaders, believe that they will enter the kingdom of heaven or be protected from what is to come if their desire is to do as they please, destroy the church, and reject and judge those who come to speak in the name of the Lord? Could these rejections, this tolerance of sin and vile acts be taking place within the religious sect in order to avoid losing members and their tithes? Have the leaders weakened because of this fear? Do they honestly believe that these actions are in conformity with the ways and will of God? The problem with the church, its leaders, and the people of this age is the lack of belief, knowledge, and understanding of God's word and their consequent lack of submission to it. Is it not yet acknowledged that God is not a respecter of persons? That he does not care about high titles or positions, but about the love, mercy, and faithfulness you show to others? Can't the church, especially its leaders, see and recognize the condition of some of its temples? Would you honestly say that this shameful condition is a trial from God, or could you sincerely admit it is of God, due to the consequences of your sinful actions and negligence, since you desired to do as you please without knowing, caring, or having the vision of what the repercussions of your actions will be? Have many of you been blinded by the pride of your high titles or positions? Now I state to all you ministers, priests, and other religious leaders: turn from your detestable ways and bring the pride of your titles down from their self-exalted religious pedestal. If you do not, I can assure you that God Himself will bring it about. First Peter 4:17 reads, "For it is time for judgment to begin at the household of God; and if it begins with us, what will be the outcome for those who do not obey the gospel of God?" Also, as Matthew 23:12 says, "And whoever exalts himself will be humbled, and he who humbles himself will be exalted."

In addition to the above, it was revealed to me that others are defiling and desecrating His temple, altars, pulpits, and holy things with the sins of fornication and adultery, greed and the misuse and improper handling of money, not giving to God what is God's but dipping their hands into the plate and taking whatever they please for their own gain. They are stealing not just from the church but from God. These are only a few of the many reasons and conditions that are keeping others away. Woe to all of you who are committing such foolishness! Have you not yet acknowledged that you are bringing judgment and dangerous consequences upon yourselves? Haven't you read that because of these present-day abominations the wrath of God is coming? "You brood of vipers! Who warned you to flee from the wrath to come?" (Matthew 3:7). How then is it possible that you are able to participate in the activities of the church, stand at the pulpits, and preach against the very same sins that you yourselves commit? Do you have no fear of God? So read and submit to God's word once again, turning from these wicked ways and repenting, for the time of judgment is not near but is already at hand. "The axe is already at the root of the trees and every tree that does not produce good fruit will be cut down and thrown into the fire" (Matthew 3:10).

Ephesians 4:1-4—I, therefore, the prisoner of the Lord, beseech you to walk worthy of the calling with which you were called, with all lowliness and gentleness, with longsuffering, bearing with one another in love, endeavoring to keep the unity of the Spirit in the bond of peace. There is one body and one Spirit, just as you were called in one hope of your calling;

Ephesians 4:28—Let him who stole steal no longer, but rather let him labor, working with his hands what is good, that he may have something to give him who has need.

1 Peter 5:2-4—Just as shepherds watch over their sheep, you must watch over everyone God has placed in your care. Do it willingly in order to please God, and not simply because you think you must. Let it be something you want to do, instead of something you do merely to make money, not domineering over those in your charge, but being examples to the flock. Then when Christ the Chief Shepherd returns, you will be given a crown that will never lose its glory. Also read 1 Timothy 6:7-11, 1 Thessalonians 5:12-15, and 1 John 3:7-10.

Therefore, in stating the above, what would it take for people, especially those within the church, to keep from their rejections, judgments, and other wrongs against one another, particularly those who bring God's word in its truth? For according to what was made known to me, not only are many churches and their leaders dealing with sin inappropriately, but they are also spiritually dead—not just spiritually asleep—because of their sins and wrongful practices. And how unfortunate that many have become lovers of themselves, with no compassion, care, or recognition of the condition and needs of others. They are concerned only with their own affairs and do not acknowledge that the Bible speaks of these very same conditions in these last days.

Matthew 24:12-13—And because lawlessness will abound, the love of many will grow cold. But he who endures to the end shall be saved. So I ask, will the lawless or undesirable act of another keep you from carrying out your kind and charitable deeds?

Ephesians 5:9-17—(for the fruit of the Spirit is in all goodness, righteousness, and truth), finding out what is acceptable to the Lord. And have no fellowship with the unfruitful works of darkness, but rather expose them. For it is shameful even to speak of those things which are done by them in secret. But all things that are exposed are made manifest by the light, for whatever makes manifest is light. Therefore He says: "Awake, you who sleep, Arise from the dead, And Christ will give you light." See then that you walk circumspectly, not as fools but as wise, redeeming the time, because the days are evil. Therefore do not be unwise, but understand what the will of the Lord is.

2 Timothy 3:1-5:—But understand this, that in the last days there will come times of difficulty. For people will be lovers of self, lovers of money, proud, arrogant, abusive, disobedient to their parents, ungrateful, unholy, heartless, unappeasable, slanderous, without self-control, brutal, not loving good, treacherous, reckless, swollen with conceit, lovers of pleasure rather than lovers of God, having the appearance of godliness, but denying its power. Avoid such people.

Matthew 25:32-46—All the nations will be gathered before Him, and He will separate them one from another, as a shepherd divides his sheep from the goats. And He will set the sheep on His right hand, but the goats on the left. Then the King will say to those on His right hand, 'Come, you blessed of My Father, inherit the kingdom prepared for you from the foundation of the world: for I was hungry and you gave Me food; I was thirsty and you gave Me drink; I was a stranger and you took Me in; I was naked and you clothed Me; I was sick and you visited Me; I was in prison and you came to Me.' "Then the righteous will answer Him, saying, 'Lord, when did we see You hungry and feed You, or thirsty and give You drink? When did we see You a stranger and take You in, or naked and clothe You? Or when did we see You sick, or in prison, and come to You?' And the King will answer and say to them, 'Assuredly, I say to you, inasmuch as you did it to one of the least of these My brethren, you did it to Me.' "Then He will also say to those on the left hand, 'Depart from Me, you cursed, into the everlasting fire prepared for the devil and his angels: for I was hungry and you gave Me no food; I was thirsty and you gave Me no drink; I was a stranger and you did not take Me in, naked and you did not clothe Me, sick and in prison and you did not visit Me.' "Then they also will answer Him, saying, 'Lord, when did we see You hungry or thirsty or a stranger or naked or sick or in prison, and did not minister to You?' Then He will answer them, saying, 'Assuredly, I say to you, inasmuch as you did not do it to one of the least of these, you did not do it to Me.' And these will go away into everlasting punishment, but the righteous into eternal life." Also read Colossians 3:12–15.

Do you honestly believe that God will turn from His judgment simply because people faithfully attend church? Or because they have claimed that it is written in the Bible, or because of their own belief? Have people become so blind that they are not able to see that the circumstances throughout the world are not normal? Have they become so hypocritical that they believe the Bible is the true word of God, but ultimately reject and deny the warnings of God's imminent Day of Judgment? How could each of these unbelieving individuals expect to be protected from any disaster if what they do is judge and reject the message brought by God's messengers? Hasn't this nation learned yet? Listen and accept, for the consequences will not fall upon anyone else except you.

Proverbs 1:7—The fear of the LORD is the beginning of knowledge, But fools despise wisdom and instruction. Also read Hosea 4:6.

Now, I ask that you be attentive to the contents of these dreams, for I found it to be of use to place them here in order to help people, religious and nonreligious alike, to grasp their meaning.

Dream 1. One day, as I was entering my office, I heard a voice calling out to me from heaven, saying: "Prepare yourself that you're ready." I responded, "I don't want to leave; there is too much work to be done here." Immediately after this, I was removed from the earth and taken up to heaven. But as I looked toward my left side, I noticed someone standing next to me. After a moment, he brought me back down to the earth, showing me people from within the church. After this, I was taken and dropped into a large and extremely deep hole that seemed to be bottomless. But after falling for some time, I came to a place that was dim and gloomy. Noticing a ledge as I looked around, I walked over to its edge and became aware of two doorways ahead of me that had volcanic lava flowing out from them. When I attempted to look further into the doorways, I was not able to, for a deep darkness that I had never seen and could never have imagined prevented me from looking any further. Then the person who was with me from the beginning came to me, pointed toward the two doorways, and said, "This is where many of them are going." I immediately woke up. Read Matthew 22:13: Then the king said to the servants, "Bind him hand and foot, take him away, and cast him into outer darkness; there will be weeping and gnashing of teeth" and Matthew 22:14: For many are called, but few are chosen. Also read Matthew 13:49 and 50, Matthew 25:30, Proverbs 16:25, and Matthew 7:12.

Dream 2. A few months later, as I saw myself entering a church, I began to notice many people of different races and denominations who were in sexual sin. As I looked up toward the back of the church, I became aware of a bright white sphere. It spoke to me: "Tell them to turn from their sins; I am giving them one more opportunity." Is there more to say about this? We all know that God detests these and many other types of sins. But I ask, for how long would God need to refrain from His wrath before people, especially those within the church, cease committing these abominations? Do you not believe that He has given the world more than its share of opportunities? Colossians 3:5: Put to death therefore what is earthly in you: sexual immorality, impurity, passion, evil desire, and covetousness, which is idolatry. Colossians 3:6: On account of these the wrath of God is coming.

Dream 3. Early in 2006, I saw myself sitting in a church, but as soon as the service began, I noticed that circus clowns were about to perform it. As eager as I was to hear the word of God, I left and entered another church. Sitting in one of the pews, I came to realize that though many people were attending, I was the only person in that pew. When I knelt to pray, a woman came to me and prayed for my eyes. As she finished, a voice began to speak to me from above.

But since the people were praising God, I was unable to hear what the voice was saying. The woman, who had left, returned and said to me, "God was attempting to speak to you, but you were unable to hear what He was saying because of the noise that came from the people." Could you honestly discern the meaning of this dream…? Hypocrites! Well did Isaiah prophesy about you, saying: "These people draw near to Me with their mouth, and honor Me with their lips, but their heart IS far from Me" (Matthew 15:7-8).

Dream 4. In this dream, as a service at a large church was about to begin, I noticed a couple of individuals pulling back a curtain from the podium (pulpit). Once it was fully opened, a group of individuals began to perform some type of dance to entertain the people. After this, I saw myself sitting on the opposite side of the pews, with a side view of the people. As I began to talk to someone about the condition of the church and its people, she ignored what I was saying and turned to talk to another person who was sitting on the other side of her. But someone sitting behind me agreed with the things that I said. During an intermission, as people left their seats, I walked to the rear of the church, where I noticed three large heaters blowing in order to warm up the people. I entered the men's restroom and saw a woman, a man washing his hands, and filth surrounding the area of the commodes. I left the restroom immediately because of my repulsion at the uncleanness. As I came to another part of the pews, I noticed a couple of computers with speaking software that is designed for use by the blind.

Revelation 3:15–18—"I know your works, that you are neither cold nor hot. I could wish you were cold or hot. So then, because you are lukewarm, and neither cold nor hot, I will vomit you out of My mouth. Because you say, 'I am rich, have become wealthy, and have need of nothing'—and do not know that you are wretched, miserable, poor, blind, and naked— I counsel you to buy from Me gold refined in the fire, that you may be rich; and white garments, that you may be clothed, that the shame of your nakedness may not be revealed; and anoint your eyes with eye salve, that you may see."

With reference to how I relate the foregoing to my experiences and observations concerning the church, I am certain that most of us can agree that in these present times, changes, spiritual downfall, and other problems have affected the church more frequently than ever before. But with reference to my own experiences, not only have I been ejected from a church, I have also been rejected by ministers and others who are acquaintances. These rejections did not stem primarily from the corrections I made known to them in accordance to what was being revealed to me, but from their skepticism about the messages I was instructed to share with the people. This should not be reason enough to prevent anyone from seeking God or attending a church, for there are several who continue to maintain and dedicate themselves to the true faith and word of God.

Nevertheless, it is imperative that the church and the people unite and bring to all the godly practices that once stood as the foundation of their life: unity, dedication, and commitment in love toward one another. But how unfortunate that a handful of church leaders have changed most of their ways! They imitate the things of the world, and are people pleasers rather than pleasers of God, eventually changing the original church and biblical practices in order to gain members. They limit God's time by the removal of personal testimonials, biblical studies, and all other essential parts of a service that help uplift and edify the spiritual life of others. Instead they dedicate the time to entertainment and singing, not realizing that a few of their members, especially their worship leaders and singers, are engaged in conflict and competition with one another rather than in service to God by meditating and singing for Him. Where, then, did the God-fearing, Bible-believing, testimony-giving, fire-preaching church of yesteryear disappear to? Read 2 Timothy 3:14–16.

2 Timothy 4:3-4—For the time is coming when people will not endure sound teaching, but having itching ears they will accumulate for themselves teachers to suit their own passions, and will turn away from listening to the truth and wander off into myths.

So, unless we recognize ourselves and repent of these ways, our past, present, and future sins still remain, for it states in James 4:7, "Submit yourselves therefore to God, resist the devil and he will flee from you." Heed these words and put them into practice in obedience to God since nobody will enter into heaven because of their own beliefs, desires, or self-righteousness. Nor can they say, "I know I'm going to heaven, I'm doing nothing wrong." How many times have I heard that statement? Don't you know we are all sinful and that religion and high titles are not the ticket to righteousness or salvation? For salvation is obtained not by attending a church or any other religious organization, as some believe, but by accepting the Lord and doing His will. Anyone and everyone commits some type of sin even while going to church, but those who desire to do good, wishing to enter into the kingdom of heaven, will follow the Lord and maintain themselves to the best of their ability. So if anyone claims to be a devoted Pentecostal, Catholic, Charismatic, Baptist, Presbyterian or an adherent of any other Christian religion and is not devoted and submissive to God's Word by showing it in love toward others, then their own devotion and faith are empty. For as the Bible states, "If anyone among you thinks he is religious, and does not bridle his tongue but deceives his own heart, this one's religion is useless. Pure and undefiled religion before God and the Father is this: to visit orphans and widows in their trouble, and to keep oneself unspotted from the world" (James 1:26-27). And Matthew 7:21 states, "Not everyone who says to me, 'Lord, Lord' will enter into the kingdom of heaven, but the one who DOES the will of my Father who is in heaven." Therefore, you must recognize that your ways may not be God's ways, for Proverbs 16:25 states, "There is a way that seems right to a man, but its end is the way to death" ("death" meaning being apart from God). So if you're one to claim that you're doing nothing wrong, consider this: do you love your neighbor as yourself, as the Bible states? Do you help your family but not others who are in need? Do you lie and always claim poverty in order to save up for yourself and yours but take (steal) from others who are in a worse condition than you are? Or are you committing one of the wrongs that are listed below? For as stated in Luke 18:19, "And Jesus said to him, 'Why do you call me "good?" No one is good except God alone.'" So if Jesus Himself stated that God alone is good, where does that leave us? You must recognize yourself, not giving in to temptation and putting off greed and the desire for more money, especially for your pleasure; lying; deception; strife; hatred (this also includes racism); cursing; pride; selfishness; jealousy; envy; stealing; homosexuality and other sexual relations/immoralities (whether one is single or married, for that constitutes fornication or adultery respectively). Lusting after someone will cause you to fall into the same sin of fornication/adultery as well. Read Matthew 25:31-46, 1 Thessalonians 5:8, and Jeremiah 2:35.

Therefore, if you do fall into one or more of these temptations, it is of utmost importance that you recognize this and repent, submitting to God on a daily basis by prayer, living according to His word and doing His will, acknowledging that we are all sinful by nature and that we all do wrong. As you begin to read your Bible, you will be able to acknowledge that these and many other wrongs are described throughout its passages. So if you're presently in or planning to enter into a relationship, I urge you to keep away from the desire to have sexual relations before marriage, or to enter into a relationship with another simply for materialistic reasons. For if your present life feels most satisfied in such ways, what guarantees a joyous one in your afterlife? In addition, married men should maintain themselves in respect, dedication, love, and faithfulness to their wives, and in like manner, married women should maintain themselves in faithfulness, trustworthiness, and loyalty to their husbands. A woman should not be a lying, money-loving, vengeful wife but a man's loving, "till-death-do-us-part" dedicated partner.

Read 1 Corinthians 7:1-5, 1 Peter 3:1, Ephesians 5:33, and Colossians 3:8.

Ephesians 4:17-25—This I say, therefore, and testify in the Lord, that you should no longer walk as the rest of the Gentiles walk, in the futility of their mind, having their understanding darkened, being alienated from the life of God, because of the ignorance that is in them, because of the blindness of their heart; who, being past feeling, have given themselves over to lewdness, to work all uncleanness with greediness. But you have not so learned Christ, if indeed you have heard Him and have been taught by Him, as the truth is in Jesus: that you put off, concerning your former conduct, the old man which grows corrupt according to the deceitful lusts, and be renewed in the spirit of your mind, and that you put on the new man which was created according to God, in true righteousness and holiness. Therefore, putting away lying, "let EACH ONE OF YOU SPEAK TRUTH WITH HIS NEIGHBOR," for we are members of one another.

It was previously stated that "religion is not the ticket to righteousness or salvation, for salvation is not obtained by attending a church or any other religious organization as some believe." However, this statement, despite its truth, should not be misunderstood in any way. It is of great importance that an individual attends and partakes in a true church of prayer, Bible study, and worship, for as the body needs nourishment, so does the spirit.

Mark 7:21–23—For from within, out of the heart of man, come evil thoughts, sexual immorality, theft, murder, adultery, coveting, wickedness, deceit, sensuality, envy, slander, pride, foolishness. All these evil things come from within, and they defile a person.

Galatians 5:19–26—Now the works of the flesh are evident: sexual immorality, impurity, sensuality, idolatry, sorcery, enmity, strife, jealousy, fits of anger, rivalries, dissensions, divisions, envy, drunkenness, orgies, and things like these. I warn you, as I warned you before, that those who do such things will not inherit the kingdom of God. But the fruit of the Spirit is: love, joy, peace [or, freedom from anxiety], patience, kindness, goodness [or, generosity], faith, gentleness [or, considerateness], self-control. Against such there is no law. Now the [ones who are] Christ's [have] crucified the flesh with its passions and its desires [or, lusts]. Since we are living in the Spirit, let us also be keeping in line with living in conformity with] the Spirit. Let us not continue becoming conceited, provoking [or, irritating] one another, envying one another!

1 Thessalonians 4:3–9—For this is the will of God, your sanctification: that you abstain from sexual immorality; that each one of you know how to control his own body in holiness and honor, not in the passion of lust like the Gentiles who do not know God; that no one transgress and wrong his brother in this matter, because the Lord is an avenger in all these things, as we told you beforehand and solemnly warned you. For God has not called us for impurity, but in holiness. Therefore whoever disregards this, disregards not man but God, who gives his Holy Spirit to you. Now concerning brotherly love you have no need for anyone to write to you, for you yourselves have been taught by God to love one another.

Romans 1:26–32—For this reason God gave them up to vile passions. For even their women exchanged the natural use for what is against nature. Likewise also the men, leaving the natural use of the woman, burned in their lust for one another, men with men committing what is shameful, and receiving in themselves the penalty of their error which was due. And even as they did not like to retain God in their knowledge, God gave them over to a debased mind, to do those things which are not fitting; being filled with all unrighteousness, sexual immorality, wickedness, covetousness, maliciousness; full of envy, murder, strife, deceit, evil-mindedness; they are whisperers, backbiters, haters of God, violent, proud, boasters, inventors of evil things, disobedient to parents, undiscerning, untrustworthy, unloving, unforgiving, unmerciful; who, knowing the righteous judgment of God, that those who practice such things are deserving of death, not only do the same but also approve of those who practice them. Also read Leviticus 20:13 and 1 Corinthians 6:9.

Revelation 21:8—But the cowardly, unbelieving, abominable, murderers, sexually immoral, sorcerers, idolaters, and all liars shall have their part in the lake which burns with fire and brimstone, which is the second death.

Chapter Twelve

THE RETURN, THE TRUTH:
A BIBLICAL AND SPIRITUAL PERSPECTIVE

The contents provided throughout this chapter may seem to represent a biblical study; you may believe that its subject will not be of concern or be of interest to you. However, the importance of its message is that it has been written to provide you with a comprehensive biblical account not only of what several churches have been omitting or unwillingly and inappropriately teaching but of the importance of the events that will soon take place.

For a vast number of years, many individuals have held on to the belief in a supernatural event that is presumed to occur sometime within the near future, an event unequal to any other since the creation of the world. This event has been widely circulated, but mainly criticized by many others throughout the world because it is to lead up to the disappearance of hundreds of thousands of people. And despite the fact that its timing is not known, Christians and other religions throughout the world continue to hold on to this belief and the truth of people being taken from this earth sometime in the near future.

Many, however, have dedicated themselves theologically to studying and eventually writing books that pertain to the Great Tribulation, focusing primarily on the second coming of the Lord (rapture), and speculating as to what point within the Bible they believe this event will take place. But the majority of the people within the church have preached, taught, and accepted that God's chosen people will be taken before the Great Tribulation (pre-tribulation), and others believe that it will happen within the three and a half years out of the seven-year tribulation (midtribulation). Still others believe that it will take place after the seven years have been completed (post-tribulation). But most do not accept the mid-tribulation or the post-tribulation rapture, since they believe that the church will be exempt from such an event, claiming without evidence that the Bible states otherwise. So in order to clarify this confusion, as well as its controversy, I have written a brief but detailed description of an approximate point within the Great Tribulation when it seems this event will take place, not from a theological point of view but from a biblical and spiritual perspective.

As you begin to reference certain books of the Old Testament, you will notice that this event was revealed to a few of the prophets, being spoken and taught with clarity by Jesus Christ Himself within the New Testament. This event was widely and boldly circulated by certain apostles, disciples, and Christians after His death and resurrection. Through their teachings they announce that this event, which many have called "the rapture," will only include those who have accepted and held on to the true faith and doctrine of Jesus Christ. However, certain individuals have misinterpreted the fourth chapter of Revelation as being the rapture of the church, simply because of what was told to John in verse 1, "come up here," believing that these words symbolize the taking of God's people. But I strongly suggest that you not quote or accept any one verse as the answer to a biblical study, since it may cause confusion or misinterpretation while referencing others on the same subject.

Nevertheless, what should be understood is that the word "rapture" is not located within any of the original translations of the Bible (KJV, NKJV, etc.), nor is it an actual biblical word. The term or word that is commonly used in conjunction with this event is called "His coming" or "the coming of the Lord." This phrase, although misinterpreted, could be found throughout several New Testament scriptures and can be referenced with the resurrection, His second coming, and the gathering together of God's people. Yet another phrase commonly used to refer to this event is "in the twinkling of an eye," which is located in 1 Corinthians 15:52 where it states, "In a moment, in the twinkling of an eye, at the last trumpet. For the trumpet will sound, and the dead will be raised incorruptible, and we shall be changed." Still another phrase that refers to this event and can also be misinterpreted is known as "the Day of the Lord," which can be found within several Old and New Testament books. But one final word that I have found to be of interest and utmost importance in describing this event is the word "Harvest." This word was mainly spoken and defined by Jesus Himself and was used as a symbol and parable of the actual "Rapture," unlike the other aforementioned terms. These references can be found in Matthew 9:37 and 38, Matthew 13:30, and Matthew 13:39, as well as Revelation 14:15 and 16.

One day, as I listened to the Bible, I heard a story in Genesis that seemed to relate to what had taken place on September 11, 2001. I acknowledge that the Book of Revelation also contains certain hidden key passages that refer to these present and end-day times, but without being able to fully relate and bring the main passages into further perspective. As I maintained myself in prayer, listening intently to the Bible while referencing certain study material, it became clearer how the order of these events will take place. Therefore, have your Bibles ready, for what I have written will give you a better understanding about what the Bible describes in reference to the 144,000 from the Tribes of the children of Israel, the gathering of God's chosen people (rapture), and on what point within the Great Tribulation it seems this event will take place. But be assured that this is not an attempt to determine a day, hour, or year of His return, or a point on the commencement of the Great Tribulation, for in Matthew 24:36 it states, "But of that day and hour no one knows, not even the angels of heaven, but My Father only."

As you now turn to Ecclesiastes 1:9, it states, "What has been is what will be, and what has been done is what will be done, and there is nothing new under the sun." Also stating in Ecclesiastes 1:10, "Is there a thing of which it is said, 'See, this is new'? It has been already in the ages before us."

Whether or not you understand the meaning of the above passages, in either case, they are merely stating what has taken place within the past and will eventually take place within the future. It is another form of saying that history repeats itself. And you may ask, What could I gather from these verses and how do they relate to what is written here? As you read certain chapters from the Old Testament, reading their events in the reverse order in which they have been presented, you will be able to get a glimpse on events that will lead up to the time of the end, eventually gaining insight into the meaning to the verses that are stated above. Therefore, beginning with Genesis chapter 11, you will read a brief description of the main content of each chapter followed by the symbolism of its events in accordance with the order of how they relate to the present and end-day times.

Genesis Chapter 11

In the beginning of this chapter, you will read a story about certain people from among the descendants of Noah who had journeyed from the East, dwelling in a land called Shinar. But one day, as they gathered together, they said to one another, "Come, let us build ourselves a city, and a tower whose top is in the heavens; let us make a name for ourselves, lest we be scattered abroad over the face of the whole earth." But according to how the story unfolds, as they were building the tower, God came down and said: "Indeed the people are one and they all have one language, and this is what they begin to do; now nothing that they propose to do will be withheld from them." "Come, let Us go down and confuse their language, that they may not understand one another's speech." So God therefore changed their language and the tower became no more, eventually scattering them abroad over the face of the whole earth.

As we now begin to look further into this chapter, you will be able to see a similarity between what had taken place during the time of the World Trade Center with what took place with the tower of Babel.

Let it be known, however, that this tower was being built in the East, within the area of Iraq, an area that is currently being rebuilt, in the same way that the World Trade Center area is now being rebuilt. What begins to get weird about this story is that the men who hijacked the planes and destroyed the World Trade Center buildings were also from the East. Another strange part to this story is that after the towers had fallen, it caused a separation of nations, similar to when God separated and scattered the people, as stated in verse 8, bringing us into a war with Iraq. Do you notice a similarity between Genesis 11 and what took place on September 11, 2001? It seems to be saying that we are now witnessing history repeating itself.

Genesis Chapter 10

In verse 2 of this chapter, you will see several names that had come from the genealogy of Noah's son Japheth—names that seem to coincide with several present-day nations that the Bible describes will go into war against Israel. The names that appear in this chapter and strangely correspond to these nations are Gomer, Magog, and Tubal (Turkey, Russia, Iran), nations that will eventually prepare for the war that is mentioned in Ezekiel 38 and 39. However, as you begin to read these chapters (Ezekiel 38 and 39), you will notice other countries that will be involved in this ultimate war as well. Despite the fact that this has not occurred yet, as you begin to enter into current events, you will see that Iran for a few years has provoked several nations, mainly the United States, with its refusal to eliminate the development of weapons of mass destruction. And another notable part to this story is that Iran, after the destruction of the World Trade Center, became more hostile and aggressive toward other nations in its refusal to comply with the disarmament of its nuclear weapons.

Genesis Chapter 9

In verse 20 of this chapter, you will notice that after the ark came to rest upon Mount Ararat, Noah decided to plant a vineyard. But after a few years had passed, he began to drink of its wine, eventually becoming naked in his tent because of his drunkenness. When his son Ham saw his Father's nakedness, he went about to tell his brothers. And after Noah learned what his son had done (Genesis 9:24), instead of placing a curse upon his son, he placed it on his grandson, Ham's son, Canaan (Genesis 9:25). And this curse seems to have been fulfilled, since the Canaanites, the descendants of Canaan, desired to have sexual relations with men who were actually angels sent by God to destroy Sodom and Gomorrah, the city in which they lived because of their wickedness (Genesis 10:19).

As we begin to look into what had taken place within this chapter, we will be able to see an act of drunkenness and of homosexuality. But aside from this, when you read verse 5, you will as well notice that God informs Noah that He will demand an account for his own "lifeblood," and from the blood of man will He demand an account for that man's blood. Could this chapter be indicating that Noah had the intention of committing suicide or murder? Or was this a message that concerns events of future times? As you begin to read and reference the passages of this story, you will find that there isn't any indication that the righteous Noah, whom God had protected from the worldwide disaster, had any desire of committing suicide or even murder. So in giving meaning to this chapter, could God have been advising Noah on what would be taking place within the future? These are homosexuality, drunkenness, murders, and suicides, occurrences that have been taking place more frequently these days than ever before.

Matthew 24:37-38—But as the days of Noah were, so also will the COMING of the Son of Man be. For as in the days before the flood, they were eating and drinking, marrying and giving in marriage, until the day that Noah entered the ark.

Genesis Chapter 8

In verse 7 of this chapter, you will see that before Noah released the dove, he first sent out a raven that flew back and forth until the water receded from the earth. However, one mysterious part to this story, which I have found to be of interest, was that the Bible does not specify the purpose of the raven and what took place as it flew about, but emphasizes the actions of the dove. As I began to look into the meaning of a raven, I was surprised to find that it was defined as a devourer and a bird of prey within the crow family. This brought me to 1 Peter 5:8, when it describes that the adversary (Satan) is like a roaring lion, seeking whom he may devour. And when you read Malachi 3:11, it states, "'And I will rebuke the devourer for your sakes, So that he will not destroy the fruit of your ground, Nor shall the vine fail to bear fruit for you in the field,' says the Lord of hosts." But as you continue to read, I am certain you will obtain a clearer understanding on the truth with regard to the symbolism of the raven and the arrival of the devourer, the Antichrist (Man of Lawlessness), which is to appear as stated in 2 Thessalonians 2 and other biblical passages that are cited throughout these paragraphs.

In reference to this chapter and on the above description, the raven, which was released before the dove, represents the one that the Bible describes as the man of perdition and lawlessness. He, who is also known to many as the Antichrist, will come upon the whole world to deceive and seek those whom he may devour. But as you read 2 Thessalonians 2 and begin to reference it with several other biblical passages, you will acknowledge that he must be revealed before God's chosen people are taken from the earth. But be advised that he, the deceiver, is active in the world in the present day, waiting for the time that God has appointed before he is able to be revealed. And although several individuals may be skeptical about this belief, as you continue to read these chapters, I am certain that you will begin to obtain a better understanding of what the Bible describes in relation to the Antichrist, the 144,000 from the Tribes of the children of Israel, and the taking up of God's chosen people.

Furthermore, I ask that you pay close attention to the events that are stated throughout these chapters, for they will include certain major occurrences within an equal number of threes, which will seem to represent and symbolize an approximate time period of His coming (rapture), during the time when the Great Tribulation is taking place.

After Noah sent out the raven, he released the dove on three separate occasions. On its first attempt, the dove returned because of its inability to find dry ground on which to rest. And on its second release, it again returned to the ark, bringing with it an olive leaf, giving Noah the indication that the water, which had covered the entire face of the earth, had begun to decrease, bringing restoration back upon the earth. But after Noah released the dove on its third attempt to determine if the flood of the waters had completely receded, the dove did not return. As I then further researched these verses, I came to the understanding that the symbolism of the dove's release represents events of the past and future final-day times.

As I looked into the symbolism of the dove's three attempts, I understood that several individuals have related its first release to the Azusa street revival of 1906, but after referencing certain other biblical passages, I came to an understanding that it could very well symbolize the Holy Spirit when it was first released by God upon those that were gathered together, as stated in Acts 2. But when the dove, on its second attempt, returned to Noah with an olive leaf, he then came to realize that the earth was in the process of being restored. This olive leaf that the dove had brought back to Noah represents the restoration of the land of Israel, which occurred in 1948. And if you recall, the dove, on its third release, did not return to Noah any longer. This last release of the dove symbolizes the removal of the Holy Spirit in the last day, when the Lord's chosen people are taken out from the earth during the three to three and a half years into the Great Tribulation. And this can be referenced with the symbolism of the raven, during the time of its release before the three attempts of the dove. Several individuals will continue to be skeptical toward this belief; however, as you continue to read along these chapters, I am certain you will come into a better understanding that what is presented throughout these paragraphs is not a form of deception or confusion, but biblical truth.

2 Thessalonians 2:1–4—Now, brethren, concerning the COMING of our Lord Jesus Christ and our gathering together to Him, we ask you, not to be soon shaken in mind or troubled, either by spirit or by word or by letter, as if from us, as though the DAY OF CHRIST had come. Let no one deceive you by any means; for that Day WILL NOT COME unless the falling away comes first, and the man of sin IS REVEALED, the son of perdition, who opposes and exalts himself above all that is called God or that is worshiped, so that he sits as God in the temple of God, showing himself that he is God.

2 Thessalonians 2:7–12—For the mystery of lawlessness is already at work; only He who now restrains will do so until He is taken out of the way. And then the lawless one will be revealed, whom the Lord will consume with the breath of His mouth and destroy with the brightness of HIS COMING. The coming of the lawless one is according to the working of Satan, with all power, signs, and lying wonders, and with all unrighteous deception among those who perish, because they did not receive the love of the truth, that they might be saved. And for this reason God will send them strong delusion, that they should believe the lie, that they all may be condemned who did not believe the truth but had pleasure in unrighteousness.

But do not be misled into believing that the verse above from 2 Thessalonians 2:7, which states, "only He who now restrains will do so until He is taken out of the way" is referring to the church or the taking (rapture) of God's people. For as we know, the church is not referred to biblically as "He" but as "she," since the "Bridegroom," who is considered to be Christ Himself, will return to receive the church as His bride. Further, if you notice, this verse is not

73

describing the church or its removal, but He who is presently restraining the lawless one, "whom the Lord will consume with the breath of His mouth and destroy with the brightness of His COMING." Also, when you read Daniel 11:31-36 and Daniel 12, you will see that God's faithful people are not resurrected (raptured) until after a time of tribulation (Daniel 12:1-3 and Daniel 12:10-12) has taken place. As you will comprehend from these chapters, His coming (rapture) will not take place until after the Antichrist is deceiving the people and the saints (the church) into accepting him and his mark, as stated in Revelation 14:9-16.

Genesis Chapters 6 and 7

As you read Genesis 6 and 7, you will come upon the story of a man named Noah, who because of his faith and obedience was chosen by God to build an ark to protect himself, his family, and the people from the worldwide catastrophe that was to come upon the earth because of the people's wickedness. But after Noah spent many years building the ark and giving fruitless warnings to the people, God, seven days prior to His judgment, instructed him to enter the ark. Then after the seven days had ended, "the fountains of the great deep were broken up and the windows of heaven were opened." As we now begin to relate this part of the story with the events of the present, it would seem to correspond to the undersea earthquake that created a large tsunami in the Indian Ocean in 2004, causing over 310,000 deaths in that region, along with the hurricane of New Orleans that took place in 2005.

As I attempted to reference these chapters with the above natural disasters, I became aware that what took place during that time did not totally relate to the story of the worldwide catastrophe of Noah. Then I recalled a dream through which I was given Revelation 3:10, which states, "Because you have kept My command to persevere, I also will keep you from the hour of trial which shall come upon the whole world, to test those who dwell on the earth." I then came to realize that if the previously written chapters are presently being fulfilled in the order in which they have been presented, and this chapter cross references with Revelation 3:10 because of their similarity to a worldwide event, then be assured that Revelation 3:10 is not too far from its fulfillment. The only difference between Revelation 3:10 and Genesis 6 and 7 is that God promised Noah that He would not destroy the whole world and all flesh by the flood of the waters. But notice, He did not promise to destroy or punish certain parts of it (haven't we noticed disasters by water?). Be reassured however, that He did promise to protect those who had persevered patiently through their trials while in His ways, just as He protected Noah and his family during the worldwide catastrophe. Therefore, keep in mind that the massive tsunami and hurricane of 2004 and 2005, although they caused many deaths and affected the whole world, were not the worldwide event that is to come, as stated in Revelation 3:10.

But according to the belief of several individuals, the phrase within Revelation 3:10 that states, "I also will keep you from the hour of trial" is considered the coming of the Lord or the taking of His people, simply because of the word "keep." Not acknowledging that the following verse states, "Behold, I am COMING quickly! Hold fast what you have, that no one may take your crown." This crown of gold of which this verse speaks will be given only to those who have been found worthy and taken at the time of His return, which seems to evidently occur after the previous verse (Revelation 3:10) has been fulfilled (Notice the word "coming"). And as I said previously, I strongly suggest that you not quote and accept any one verse as the answer to a biblical study, since it may cause confusion or misinterpretation while referencing others within the same subject.

Revelation 22:12—"And behold, I am COMING quickly, and My reward is with Me, to give to every one according to his work." Also Read Revelation 22:20.

1 Corinthians 15:23—But each one in his own order: Christ the first fruits, afterward those who are Christ's AT HIS COMING.

In the below paragraph, you will read of a dream that I received a couple of years ago that can also be located within the "Prophetic Revelation" section, chapter 6, finding its contents to be of interest and of utmost importance to place here because of its relation to a worldwide event that is to occur as described in Revelation 3:10.

One day as I was about to enter a church, I noticed that it was full. After I had waited outside for some time, the crowd gathered around the entrance allowed me to enter. As I was walking down the aisle, the preacher began to pray for me. When he finished, I noticed that I was standing in front of the podium (pulpit) overlooking the many people who were attending the service. Suddenly, I heard a voice that said to me, "Write the ten plagues of the Bible on ten pieces of paper." Two men came and began to assist me in writing the plagues, placing the papers in the offering plate. After the plagues were written, the voice, which I had known to be the Spirit of God, spoke to me again and said, "Now have nine people select nine out of the ten papers." But when I began to inform the people what the Spirit of God was instructing me to do, many began to leave because of their unbelief, and the church was left half empty. Now, as the offering plate was being passed, nine people randomly selected the papers as they had been instructed. The two men returned and handed me the offering plate. As I brought the remaining paper to eye level, the Spirit of God said to me, "This is the last plague I am going to send down to the earth." Again, when I shared this message with the people, many more began to leave because of their lack of belief. As I turned toward the ministers, they laughed and rejected me, saying, "God would not do or say such things." However, this dream could not be more true, for as soon as I began to share this message with the people, many refused to believe. I was amazed by their lack of acceptance. Many of these people claimed to believe in God and His word, but undoubtedly lacked spiritual knowledge and biblical understanding. This brings to mind the story of Noah, in which the people refused to believe the message until judgment came, and by then it was too late. In prayer I asked God for a confirmation, and after a few days I received Revelation 3:10, which says, "Because you have kept My command to persevere, I also will keep you from the hour of trial which shall come upon the whole world, to test those who dwell on the earth. For further study of the ten plagues of the Bible, read Exodus, chapters 8 through 12.

Then, one evening as I was in prayer, the above dream dwelled in my mind, but while I was in deep thought, Revelation 3:10 (the worldwide event) and Exodus 12:29 (the last plague that came upon Egypt) simultaneously came to mind. But as I maintained myself in prayer, referencing these verses with Exodus 9:13 (the locusts that devoured the crops), Exodus 9:21 and 22 (three days of darkness), Exodus 12:29 (the angel of death), and the raven of Genesis 8, which also symbolizes death and was released by Noah before the three attempts of the dove, I came to realize that the above dream could very well represent the arrival of the Antichrist himself: the reason being that if you look into the last three plagues of the Bible, they seem to describe the same three events that must take place before God's people are taken from the earth, just as the Israelites were evidently taken out of Egypt after three days and after the three last plagues were fulfilled.

As you now look into what took place in the first plague, which was actually the eighth, you will see that God sent a swarm of locusts in order to devour the crops in Egypt (Exodus 10:4, 5, 12–15). As we all know, when locusts come to devour the crops, they bring a devastation that shortens the food supply and eventually causes a famine. This plague has not occurred yet, whether through locusts, any other insect, or a disaster of any sort, but according to the rate of our economy, the treatment of our food supply, and what was made known to me, I am certain that we are not too far from its fulfillment.

Note: According to a report from the American Beekeeper Federation, there has been an unexplained collapse of beehives in the country and the world, with entire colonies being wiped out. Maryann Frazier, apiculture extension associate at Penn State University says, "Since the beginning of the year beekeepers from all over the country have been reporting unprecedented losses. The losses are staggering: one beekeeper lost 11,000 of his 13,000 colonies; another virtually all of his 10,000. The problem is so large that beekeepers are starting to wonder if their industry can survive. A beekeeper told the farmers that their farms might go under if the bees were wiped out. Are we facing a collapse of our food production? We just don't know how widespread it is or how soon it will have a major impact on our worldwide food supply. Be assured, the problems are coming, and they're going to get worse, whether it's the end of honeybees or a parallel calamity."

Albert Einstein once said, "If the bee disappeared off the surface of the globe, then man would have only four years of life left." And you may ask, why? Because without bees, plants don't get pollinated, and without pollination, say good-bye to fruits, nuts, and some vegetables. We won't have natural oils (such as olive oil or sunflower oil). We also won't have many natural fibers. You can see how important the bee is to our livelihood and existence.

Immediately during the time of the famine (economic collapse), we come to the next plague that will be three days of darkness (Exodus 10:22). These three days represent the three to three and a half years of worldwide economic collapse followed by the arrival of the last plague, which is the devourer/destroyer (Exodus 12:23) or better known as the Antichrist, which came upon the Egyptians before the Israelites were taken out of Egypt. But as you read Exodus 12:21–23, you will notice that in order for the Israelites to be protected from the last plague, it was necessary for them to have the blood of a lamb placed on three places of their doors. This blood, as several of us may know, represents the blood of Christ, the Lamb of God who protects and takes away the sin of the world. Not only are these events giving us a preview of what is to take place in the last days, but look at the symbolism of every event and how they carry a set of equal number of threes, and how they relate to a time of tribulation and His return.

Furthermore, if you reference and compare the first two plagues with the third seal of Revelation 6:5–6 (the black horse that represents the darkness of economic collapse and famine), then you will be able to see that not only do they relate and reference with one another, but they as well carry a set equal number of threes, a possible symbolic time when the people will be forced and deceived into taking the mark of the beast in order for them to be able to buy and sell (Revelation 13). When you turn to Matthew 27:45 and Mark 15:33, you will again notice a darkness that comes over the whole land for three hours. And in Mark 15:27, you will see that Christ was crucified with two other men, bringing the total number to three.

Revelation 6:5-6—When He opened the third seal, I heard the third living creature say, "Come and see." So I looked, and behold, a black horse, and he who sat on it had a pair of scales in his hand. And I heard a voice in the midst of the four living creatures saying, "A quart of wheat for a denarius, and three quarts of barley for a denarius; and do not harm the oil and the wine."

Mark 15:33—Now when the sixth hour had come, there was darkness over the whole land until the ninth hour.

But another example can be read in Daniel 3, when King Nebuchadnezzar made and set up an image of gold that was ninety feet high and nine feet long and that the people were forced to worship. But three of God's servants—Shadrach, Meshach, and Abed-Nego—refused to worship the Image, the King ordered that they be killed by being thrown into the fiery furnace. Now, as you look into the height and width of the image and divide that first number into three parts, of course, it divides into an equal number of 3 or 30 (30x3). In so like manner, when you divide the width of the image by three, it will again give you a set number of threes (3x3). And though several of these analogies may not necessarily have any relevance to the set time of the Great Tribulation or His coming, one of the reasons I have included them within these paragraphs is for the reader to grasp an insight into how these events strangely reference the set number of threes. Nevertheless, as you read this and the above passage in Daniel 3, notice the similarity between this part of the story and what will happen to those who refuse to worship the beast and his image, during the time of the Great Tribulation in Daniel 11:31–36 and Revelation 13:15.

Daniel 11:31-36—He will send troops to pollute the temple and the fortress, and he will stop the daily sacrifices. Then he will set up that "Horrible Thing" that causes destruction. The king will use deceit to win followers from those who are unfaithful to God, but those who remain faithful will do everything possible to oppose him. Wise leaders will instruct many of the people. But for a while, some of these leaders will either be killed with swords or burned alive, or else robbed of their possessions and thrown into prison. They will receive only a little help in their time of trouble, and many of their followers will be treacherous. Some of those who are wise will suffer, so that God will make them pure and acceptable until the end, which will still come at the time He has decided. This king will do as he pleases. He will proudly claim to be greater than any god and will insult the only true God. Indeed, he will be successful until God is no longer angry with His people.

Revelation 13:15—He was granted power to give breath to the image of the beast, that the image of the beast should both speak and cause as many as would not worship the image of the beast to be killed.

A couple of other examples can be located in Luke 4:25, where it states: "But I tell you truly, many widows were in Israel in the days of Elijah, when the heaven was shut up three years and six months, and there was a great famine throughout all the land." Have you noticed the famine of over three years as described in the last three plagues of Exodus? Again, if you turn to Revelation 11:11, you will see that two of God's servants (prophets) are killed, but were not raised from the dead and taken up to heaven until after the three and a half days had past. But notice verse 12, and how it seems to represent and symbolize the time when God's chosen people are called and taken from the earth (raptured).

Revelation 11:9—Then those from the peoples, tribes, tongues, and nations will see their dead bodies three-and-a-half days, and not allow their dead bodies to be put into graves.

Revelation 11:11-12—Now after the three and a half days the breath of life from God entered them, and they stood on their feet, and great fear fell on those who saw them. And they heard a loud voice from heaven saying to them, "Come up here." And they ascended to heaven in a cloud, and their enemies saw them.

Other interesting passages that closely relate to this event with the symbolism of the number three can be located in Hosea 6:2, where it states: "After two days He will revive us; on the third day He will raise us up, that we may live in His sight." And yet, a few other passages that can be related with these events are in Jonah 1:17 and Matthew 12:40, of Jonah in the darkness while in the belly of a great fish for three days and three nights; Matthew 16:21, telling of Jesus being raised on the third day; Mark 15:25, of Jesus being crucified on the third hour (also read Mark 15:27 and Mark 15:33); Luke 9:22; Acts 10:40; 1 Corinthians 15:4, the resurrection of Jesus taking place on the third day; 2 Corinthians 12:2, in which Paul describes an event that had taken place in the third heaven. And if you recall, Jesus began His ministry at the age of thirty, and was crucified three to three and a half years after His ministry began, bringing the trinity of the Father, the Son, and the Holy Spirit.

As you read the following passages, you will be able to notice the events that are taking place on the third day and how closely they relate with the coming of the Lord and the taking up of God's people, as stated in Matthew 24:29–31 and Mark 13:25–27.

Exodus 19:10-11—Then the LORD said to Moses, "Go to the people and consecrate them today and tomorrow, and let them wash their clothes. And let them be ready for the third day. For on the third day the LORD will come down upon Mount Sinai in the sight of all the people." (These passages can also be referenced with Matthew 24:30, Mark 13:26 and 27, and Luke 21:27 and 28.)

Exodus 19:16—Then it came to pass on the third day, in the morning, that there were thunderings and lightnings, and a thick cloud on the mountain; and the sound of the trumpet was very loud, so that all the people who were in the camp trembled.

Exodus 19:20—Then the LORD came down upon Mount Sinai, on the top of the mountain. And the LORD called Moses to the top of the mountain, and Moses went up. (Doesn't this verse also seem to represent the coming of the Lord and the taking up (rapture) of God's people?)

Furthermore, if you reference the below passages with Revelation 3:10-11, along with 2 Thessalonians 2 and Revelation 6:9-12, then it will seem evident that the worldwide event stated in Revelation 3:10 represents the arrival of the lawless one, also known by many as the Antichrist, who will come upon the whole world to deceive those who live on the earth, before the COMING of the Lord. But I ask that you pay close attention to the capitalized word (coming) within these passages, for it will give evidence supporting the belief in the events of the Great Tribulation, before the time of His COMING. However, keep in mind that the above dream can also represent a worldwide economic collapse followed by a famine, which is the open door for the arrival of the lawless one as I have described throughout this chapter. This economic collapse will allow him to take the opportunity to deceive the people into accepting him and his mark, for this will be their only means of surviving hunger and death. Many believe they will not accept but refuse this mark, but when they read 2 Thessalonians 2:10–12 and look into the definition of the word "deceive" or "deception," they will acknowledge that according to its description, there may not be any choice or decision in this matter. For "deceive," "mislead," "delude," and "beguile" mean to lead astray or frustrate, usually by underhandedness. Deceive implies imposing a false idea or belief that causes ignorance, bewilderment, or helplessness. Delude means deceiving so thoroughly as to obscure the truth; "we were deluded into thinking we were safe." Beguile stresses the use of charm and persuasion in deceiving ("was beguiled by false promises"). Also reference the below passages with 1 Corinthians 15:23.

Matthew 24:3–24—Now as He sat on the Mount of Olives, the disciples came to Him privately, saying, "Tell us, when will these things be? And what will be the sign of Your COMING, and of the end of the age?" And Jesus answered and said to them: "Take heed that no one deceives you. For many will come in My name, saying, 'I am the Christ,' and will deceive many. And you will hear of wars and rumors of wars. See that you are not troubled; for all these things must come to pass, but the end is not yet. For nation will rise against nation, and kingdom against kingdom. And there will be famines, pestilences, and earthquakes in various places. All these are the beginning of sorrows. Then they will deliver you up to tribulation and kill you, and you will be hated by all nations for My name's sake. And then many will be offended, will betray one another, and will hate one another. Then many false prophets will rise up and deceive many. And because lawlessness will abound, the love of many will grow cold. But he who endures to the end shall be saved. And this gospel of the kingdom will be preached in all the world as a witness to all the nations, and then the end will come. Therefore when you see the 'ABOMINATION OF DESOLATION,' spoken of by Daniel the prophet, standing in the holy place (whoever reads, let him understand), then let those who are in Judea flee to the mountains. Let him who is on the housetop not go down to take anything out of his house. And let him who is in the field not go back to get his clothes. But woe to those who are pregnant and to those who are nursing babies in those days! And pray that your flight may not be in winter or on the Sabbath. For then there will be Great

Tribulation, such as has not been since the beginning of the world until this time, no, nor ever shall be. And unless those days were shortened, no flesh would be saved; but for the elect's sake those days will be shortened. Then if anyone says to you, 'Look, here is the Christ!' or 'There!' do not believe it. For false Christs and false prophets will rise and show great signs and wonders to deceive, if possible, even the elect." Read Daniel 11:31.

Matthew 24:29–31—"Immediately AFTER THE TRIBULA-TION of those days the sun will be darkened, and the moon will not give its light; the stars will fall from heaven, and the powers of the heavens will be shaken. Then the sign of the Son of Man will appear in heaven, and then all the tribes of the earth will mourn, and they will see the Son of Man COMING on the clouds of heaven with power and great glory (Revelation 14:1–16). And He will send His angels with a great sound of a trumpet, and they will gather together His elect from the four winds, from one end of heaven to the other." (Also reference this with Revelation 6:12– 17.)

Matthew 24:37-40—"But as the days of Noah were, so also will the COMING of the Son of Man be." For as in the days before the flood, they were eating and drinking, marrying and giving in marriage, until the day that Noah entered the ark, and did not know until the flood came and took them all away, so also will the COMING of the Son of Man be. Then two men will be in the field: one will be taken and the other left."

Matthew 24:42—"Watch therefore, for you do not know what hour your Lord is COMING."

Matthew 24:44—"Therefore you also be ready, for the Son of Man is COMING at an hour you do not expect."

Acts 2:19–21—"I will show wonders in heaven above and signs in the earth beneath: Blood and fire and vapor of smoke. The sun shall be turned into darkness, and the moon into blood (Revelation 6:12), BEFORE THE COMING of the great and awesome DAY OF THE LORD. And it shall come to pass that whoever calls on the name of the Lord shall be saved." (Also reference with Matthew 24:29-31 and Joel 2:31.)

As you now read the following passages from Daniel 11 and 12, notice the capitalized words and how they seem to determine a time BEFORE Christ's coming. For as we know, it is biblically evident that "those who remain faithful" to God will be among the worthy who will be EVENTUALLY taken (raptured) from the earth.

Daniel 11:31-36—He will send troops to pollute the temple and the fortress, and he will stop the daily sacrifices. Then he will set up that "Horrible Thing" that causes destruction. The king will USE DECEIT to win followers from those who are UNFAITHFUL to God, but THOSE WHO REMAIN FAITHFUL will do everything possible to oppose him. Wise leaders will instruct many of the people. But for a while, some of these leaders will either be killed with swords or burned alive, or else robbed of their possessions and thrown into prison. They will receive only a little help in their time of trouble, and many of their followers will be treacherous. Some of those who are wise will suffer, so that God will make them PURE AND ACCEPTABLE UNTIL THE END, which will still come at the time He has decided. This king will do as he pleases. He will proudly claim to be greater than any god and will insult the only true God. Indeed, he will be successful UNTIL GOD IS NO LONGER ANGRY WITH HIS PEOPLE.

Daniel 12:1-4—"At that time Michael shall stand up, The great prince who stands watch over the sons of your people; And there shall be A TIME OF TROUBLE, such as never was since there was a nation, Even to that time. And at that time your people shall be delivered, every one who is found written in the book. And MANY OF THOSE WHO SLEEP IN THE DUST OF THE EARTH

SHALL AWAKE, some to everlasting life, some to shame and everlasting contempt. Those who are wise shall shine Like the brightness of the firmament, and those who turn many to righteousness like the stars forever and ever. "But you, Daniel, shut up the words, and seal the book until the time of the end; many shall run to and fro, and knowledge shall increase."

Daniel 12:6-7—And one said to the man clothed in linen, who was above the waters of the river, "How long shall the fulfillment of these wonders be?" Then I heard the man clothed in linen, who was above the waters of the river, when he held up his right hand and his left hand to heaven, and swore by Him who lives forever, that it shall be for A TIME, TIMES, AND HALF A TIME (3 and a half years); and when the power of the holy people has been completely shattered, ALL these things shall be finished.

In like manner, as we turn again to Revelation 3:10 and begin to relate it with Genesis 7 along with Exodus 12, then you will notice a similarity between these passages, since they seem to correspond to a protection in one way or another. Revelation 3:10 states that because you have kept his command to persevere patiently in your trials, He will therefore protect you from what is to come upon the whole world. In Genesis, Noah, because he endured for many years in the ways of God, was protected from the worldwide catastrophe. And in Exodus, the Israelites, who had endured harsh trials for many years, were protected from the destroyer, which was the last plague that God had brought upon the whole land of Egypt (Exodus 11:1 and 12:23) because of their obedience in placing the blood of a lamb on their homes. As stated previously, the blood of the lamb represents the Lord, the one who takes away the sin of the world (John 1:29 and 36), who protects and keeps those in the hour of trial.

Genesis Chapters 4 and 5
As we now turn to Genesis chapters 4 and 5, you will find several unusual and extraordinary events that many have expected for the

near future but misinterpreted. But I ask that you be attentive to the description and biblical passages that are stated below, for they will broaden your understanding with regard to those who will be redeemed from the earth, the first as well as the second resurrection, and the time during the Great Tribulation.

When you begin to read Genesis 4 and 5, it would seem to describe the taking or disappearance of God's people (Genesis 5:24 before the arrival of the mark; Genesis 4:15), which is to come during the time of the Great Tribulation. But as I then began to read and reference several biblical chapters, I came to realize that chapter 4 could as well be combined (read in its proper order) with chapter 5, since it is biblically evident that the disappearance of God's people, which many have referred to as the rapture, will take place simultaneously with the dead during the three to three and a half years out of the seven-year Great Tribulation. This seems to happen during the time when the people will be deceived into accepting the mark of the beast and his image, as described throughout these passages. Nevertheless, when you read the description from Genesis 5, then 4, you will notice that its contents could very well symbolize and correspond, not to His coming (rapture), but to those who will be redeemed from the earth as described below.

Now, as you turn to Genesis 4, you will find a story that involves two brothers, Cain and Abel. As the story goes, they were both in the field; Cain became angry and eventually killed his brother because God had considered Abel's offering more favorable than his. But as God knew of what he had done, He decided to place a curse upon him and drive him out from the land. Since Cain felt that his punishment was more than he could bear, he therefore complained to God because of the fear of being driven out from the land and killed by the people. So God decided to "set a mark on Cain," driving him out from the land in which he was and out from His presence.

As you look closely into the events of this chapter (Genesis 4), and reference it with Lucifer's fall from heaven along with the events of the Great Tribulation, then you will be able to determine a similarity between them. First, Cain becomes jealous at the righteous act of his brother Abel; Lucifer becomes envious and jealous of God; Cain becomes angry and kills his brother; and Lucifer is angry at God's righteous people and begins to kill them in the Book of Revelation. Cain has a mark set upon him; Lucifer begins to place a mark on people at the time of his deception; Cain is driven out from the land; and Lucifer is also driven out from heaven because of what he has done. However, the main concept of this story is that Cain, who becomes angry because of the righteous act of another, deceives his brother and kills him; a mark is then set on him. Doesn't this seem to coincide with the events that are to occur in the Great Tribulation as described in Revelation 14 and 20?

In Genesis 5 beginning with verse 24, you will read a couple of biblical passages that involve a man named Enoch, who in his earlier years begins to walk with God. But after many years of walking in the ways of righteousness, Enoch, because of his uprightness, is suddenly taken out from the earth. And if you notice, the Bible does not describe the taking of Enoch as a form of death, but as a disappearance. And this chapter seems to symbolize and represent the taking of god's people in two forms; in the first, as you read Revelation 14:3 and 4, you will see that the 144,000 from the Tribes of the children of Israel will be redeemed from the earth before the taking (rapture) of God's people (Revelation 14:14–16). And despite that, several if not many will reject this belief; however, when you turn to Revelation 14:3–4, you will notice that these 144,000 "were" (notice the words of past tense) redeemed from the earth before God's people had been "reaped" (rapture) from the earth (Revelation 14:15 and 16). And yet, as you read Genesis 1:4 and 14-18, you will see that God, divides the light from the darkness. These two events, if used in the context as described in this paragraph, seem to give us a symbolism of when God, on two separate occasions, separates the righteous people from the wicked. The first separation will be of those from the 144,000 from the Tribes of the children of Israel. Then after this, during the three to three and a half years into the great Tribulation, will be those who will be taken at Christ's coming, which is the time of the first resurrection (1 Thessalonians 4:15–17 and Revelation 14:15 and 16). And the evidence for this belief can be found in 1 Corinthians 15:23, where it states, "But each one in his own order: Christ the firstfruits, afterward those who are Christ's at His COMING." And this verse also gives evidence to these 144,000, since they themselves were considered "firstfruits" as stated in Revelation 14:4. Therefore, if these 144,000 were considered "firstfruits" to God and of Christ, being found to be blameless in all things (Revelation 14:4 and 5), then could we honestly believe that these 144,000 who "are without fault before the throne of God (Revelation 14:5) would be left behind, while the other chosen people were taken out (raptured) from the earth, as some have believed? Besides, when you read Revelation 14:1, then you will notice that God appears on the mountain with the 144,000 before His COMING and the taking (rapture) of His people as stated in Revelation 14:15 and 16.

As you begin to reference Revelation 14 and 20, it will seem evident that only one redemption and two resurrections will occur. This redemption will only include those from the 144,000 from the Tribes of the children of Israel as described in Revelation 14:1-3. And those who will take part in the first resurrection will be those as described in Daniel 12:1 and 2, 1 Thessalonians 4:15–17, Revelation 14:14-16, and Revelation 20. But those who were not taken in the first will unfortunately take part in the second resurrection because of their unworthiness or because they have eventually taken the mark of the beast or of his image. These will be those who face the danger of the second death (lake of fire) as described in Revelation 20:10-15. But notice how the number three appears in these passages as well: redemption, the first and second resurrections, and the beast, his image, and the Antichrist.

1 Thessalonians 4:15–17—For this we say to you by the word of the Lord, that we who are alive and remain until the COMING of the Lord will by no means precede those who are asleep. For the Lord Himself will descend from heaven with a shout, with the voice of an archangel, and with the trumpet of God. And the dead in Christ will rise first. Then we who are alive and remain shall be caught up together with them in the clouds to meet the Lord in the air. And thus we shall always be with the Lord.

As we then look into Revelation 14:8, you will read of a place that many have considered, according to its biblical description, to be New York City: a city that by its economic riches and luxurious living has kept many nations throughout the world from an economic downfall. However, as soon as New York's economic market comes to its ultimate demise, the United States along with the rest of the world will without a doubt come into a Great Depression worse than the one that took place in 1929. This economic collapse, according to biblical description and prophecy, will be the last economic downfall before the appearance of the lawless one (Antichrist). But how unfortunate that many have disregarded this belief, not acknowledging that the deficits, corruption and overspending taking place throughout many local, city, state, and federal agencies, along with the lack of employment and higher prices for clothing, medicines, insurance, oil, gasoline, food products, etc., will be among the causes that will eventually lead up to the economic downfall and the other events. Read Revelation 14:8 and Revelation 17:5.

Therefore, if you have paid close attention to the order of these events, referencing them with those from the three last plagues of Exodus, you will have seen a striking resemblance between the fall of Babylon the Great (economic collapse/famine) followed by the appearance of the lawless one as stated in Exodus 10:22 (three days of darkness) and Exodus 12:23 (the last plague that was the arrival of the destroyer), followed by the coming of the Lord (rapture) as referenced in Genesis 18. Are you now able to see a pattern to these events and those that will be taking place during the time of the end?

Nevertheless, as you read Revelation 14:9–12, you will see that a third angel is advising and warning the saints of the consequences of accepting the mark of the beast and his image. And this verse is not intended as a warning toward the Tribes from the 144,000, for if you turn to Revelation 7:3 and 4, you will notice that an angel advises four other angels not to harm the earth "until we have Sealed the servants of our God on their foreheads." This seal, which was placed on the 144,000, is not necessarily a seal to protect them from death, but for the purpose of their protection in order to set them apart for God, since they are the "firstfruits" of Christ who "were redeemed" from the earth as described in Revelation 14:3-5, clearly giving us the indication that these 144,000 will not be receiving the mark of the beast and his image. So then, could there be any other saints to which this verse could be referring if one has already been sealed and redeemed by the angels of God? Aren't the multitude of Revelation 7:9 considered saints as well? Isn't this a warning for these other chosen people of God (the church)? Therefore, in evaluating and referencing these and other passages from the Bible, it is evident that the church, despite its rejections and beliefs, will not be "taken" (raptured) until during the time when the mark of the beast and his image are placed upon the people as described in Revelation 14:9–16.

Revelation 14:3-5—They sang as it were a new song before the throne, before the four living creatures, and the elders; and no one could learn that song except the hundred and forty-four thousand who WERE REDEEMED from the earth. These are the ones who were not defiled with women, for they are virgins. These are the ones who follow the Lamb wherever He goes. These WERE REDEEMED from among men, BEING FIRSTFRUITS to God and to the Lamb. And in their mouth was found no deceit, for they are without fault before the throne of God.

Revelation 14:9–12—Then a THIRD angel followed them, saying with a loud voice, "If anyone worships the beast and his image, and receives his mark on his forehead or on his hand, he himself shall also drink of the wine of the wrath of God, which is poured out full strength into the cup of His indignation. He shall be tormented with fire and brimstone in the presence of the holy angels and in the presence of the Lamb. And the smoke of their torment ascends forever and ever; and they have no rest day or night, who worship the beast and his image, and whoever receives the mark of his name." Here is the patience of the SAINTS; here are those who keep the commandments of God and the faith of Jesus.

But when you turn to Revelation 14:14, you will read of when John sees one who looks like a "Son of man," sitting on a white cloud and wearing a crown of gold, Who as most of us may know is Christ Himself, for as you read the following passages, you will notice when He (the Lord) reaps of the earth's harvest as stated in Mathew 9:37 and 38, Mathew 13:30 and 39, and Mark 4:29 and Luke 10:2.

Revelation 14:14–16—Then I looked, and behold, a white cloud, and on the cloud sat One like the Son of Man, having on His head a golden crown, and in His hand a sharp sickle. And another angel came out of the temple, crying with a loud voice to Him who sat on the cloud, "Thrust in Your sickle and reap, for the time has come for You to reap, for the harvest of the earth is ripe." So He who sat on the cloud thrust in His sickle on the earth, and the earth was reaped.

Furthermore, when you turn to the verses that are stated in the following paragraph, notice the word "blessed" and how it seems to be giving us the evidence of the event of the Great Tribulation, with regard to the hope of those "who waits" forty-five days after the daily sacrifice has been abolished and the abomination of desolation is set up. Could the forty-five-day time period of the "Blessed" "who waits" be referring to the time of the coming of the Lord (rapture)? As you reference these passages along with those in Revelation 14, 20, and 19, it will seem evident that it is describing the expectancy of that hope. Daniel 12:11 states, "And from the time that the daily sacrifice is taken away, and the abomination of desolation is set up, there shall be one thousand two hundred and ninety days." Daniel 12:12 says, "Blessed is he who waits, and comes to the one thousand three hundred and thirty-five days." And Revelation 14:13 states, "Blessed are the dead who die in the Lord from now on." "Yes, says the Spirit, that they may rest from their labors, and their works follow them." Then Revelation 20:6 states, "Blessed and holy is he who has part in the first resurrection. Over such the second death has no power, but they shall be priests of God and of Christ, and shall reign with Him a thousand years." And again, in Revelation 19:9: "Then He said to me, 'Write: "Blessed are those who are called to the marriage supper of the Lamb!"' And He said to me, 'These are the true sayings of God.'" Could we now see and acknowledge that these passages seem to describe that these "Blessed" "who waits" for the forty-five-day period during the time of the Great Tribulation will be of those who will be taken (raptured) and resurrected from the earth? But as you turn to Revelation 5, you will notice that the four living creatures along with the twenty-four elders are holding bowls of incense: the prayers of the saints. These prayers that the creatures and elders are holding are without a doubt those from the 144,000 from the Tribes of the children of Israel. For if you reference Revelation 5:8 with Revelation 14:3, you will realize that the 144,000 are those that are singing a "New Song" before the throne, before the living creatures and the elders.

Revelation 5:8–10—Now when He had taken the scroll, the four living creatures and the twenty-four elders fell down before the Lamb, each having a harp, and golden bowls full of incense, which are the prayers of the saints. And they sang a new song, saying: "You are worthy to take the scroll, And to open its seals; For You were slain, And have redeemed us to God by Your blood Out of every tribe and tongue and people and nation, and have made us kings and priests to our God; And we shall reign on the earth."

Revelation 14:3—They sang as it were a new song before the throne, before the four living creatures, and the elders; and no one

93

could learn that song except the hundred and forty-four thousand who were redeemed from the earth.

In Addition to the above, when you read Revelation 8 beginning with verses 3–5, you will notice that "another angel, having a golden censer, came and stood at the altar. He was given much incense that he should offer it with the prayers of ALL the saints upon the golden altar which was before the throne. And the smoke of the incense, with the prayers of the saints, ascended before God from the angel's hand. Then the angel took the censer, filled it with fire from the altar, and threw it to the earth. And there were noises, thunderings, lightnings, and an earthquake." As we begin to look closer into the events of these passages, it will seem they describe that "the prayers of all the saints" (Redeemed as well as the resurrected) will no longer be necessary since the people who had maintained themselves patiently in the ways of God will now be able to speak with Him directly. For prayers are not required when one has entered into the kingdom of heaven but are necessary when attempting to communicate with God while still living on the earth. Therefore, since the redemption and His coming will be accomplished by the opening of the seventh seal (see the closing of this chapter), the smoke of the incense, with the prayers of all the saints, will not be required and will therefore ascend before God from the angel's hand. Read Revelation 8:6.

Genesis Chapter 3
As we now turn to Genesis 3, you will be able to see a similarity between the fall and curse of the serpent with that of the fall of Satan, that serpent of old as described in Revelation 20. But when you read these first three chapters of Genesis, notice how they strongly resemble and coincide with the last three chapters of Revelation. In the beginning verses of this chapter, you will see that the serpent uses deception in attempts to persuade Eve into the eating of a fruit, which God had prohibited them to touch or eat. However, when you turn to Genesis 2:17, you will notice that the serpent in Genesis 3 was not contrary to what God had stated, but

informing her that the forbidden fruit will not cause her physical death but allow her to have the ability to be like God Himself, knowing good and evil (Genesis 3:5). And as the story continues, Eve eventually falls into his deception, desires the fruit, eats, and gives it to her husband, Adam, who begins to eat as well (Genesis 3:6). However, doesn't it seem somewhat peculiar that the number three of this chapter, which corresponds to a time of Satan's deception, also relates to the time when he is deceiving the people, during the three to three and a half years into the Great Tribulation?

Genesis 3:1–7—Now the serpent was more cunning than any beast of the field which the LORD God had made. And he said to the woman, "Has God indeed said, 'You shall not eat of every tree of the garden'?" And the woman said to the serpent, "We may eat the fruit of the trees of the garden; but of the fruit of the tree which is in the midst of the garden, God has said, 'You shall not eat it, nor shall you touch it, lest you die.'" Then the serpent said to the woman, "You will not surely die. For God knows that in the day you eat of it your eyes will be opened, and you will be like God, knowing good and evil." So when the woman saw that the tree was good for food, that it was pleasant to the eyes, and a tree desirable to make one wise, she took of its fruit and ate. She also gave to her husband with her, and he ate. Then the eyes of both of them were opened, and they knew that they were naked; and they sewed fig leaves together and made themselves coverings.

But the main focus of this chapter is that the serpent, because of his craftiness, fell due to the curse that was placed upon him by God for deceiving mankind and bringing about its fall (Genesis 3). And this chapter seems to symbolize and closely relate to the fall of Satan (the deceiver) who will be finally bound and thrown into the lake of fire because of his deception as described in Revelation 20.

Genesis Chapters 1 and 2

After the curse and the fall of the serpent (Genesis 3 and Revelation 20), we now come to the last two chapters of Genesis that will bring the beginning of these events to its ultimate end. But as you reference these chapters with those from Revelation 21 and 22, you will be able to see that what was created in the beginning coincides with what will be in the time of the end.

In the beginning, the light that God had brought about in Genesis 1 will be the light that will come from His presence (Revelation 21:23) when the great city, the New Jerusalem, comes down from heaven after He gathers His people from the darkness of the earth. This place, which will descend from heaven (Revelation 21:2 and 21:10) will be adorned with gold and precious stones. A river of life will flow through it, and a tree of life that will bear twelve fruits will also be present. In that day, He will dwell with His people and wipe every tear from their eyes; there will be no death, sorrow, or pain, just as it was during the time before the fall of Adam and Eve. Do you now see the similarity between what was in the time of the creation and what will be in the time of the end? (A river of life, a Tree of Life, fruits, no pain, no sorrows, gold and precious stones.)

If you reference the seventh day when God had ended his creation (Genesis 2) with that of the last seal, bowl, and trumpet (Revelation 6, 8, and 16), you will be able to determine a striking similarity between these events:

In Genesis 1, you will see that God, on the first day of creation, said "let there be Light," creating the world in six days. But on the seventh day, since all that He had created was completed, He therefore rested from the six days of His creation (Genesis 2:2 and 3), stating that all He had made was very good (Genesis 1:31). However, as you read the last book of the Bible, the Book of Revelation, you will notice times of distress and trouble because the world has become dark and sinful; now, rather than being in light, it will be in darkness. And because of this, God will pour out His wrath upon the earth, bringing seven seals (Revelation 6), seven angels to sound seven trumpets (Revelation 8:6, 9 and Revelation 11:15), and seven bowls of God's wrath (Revelation 16), which will be poured out upon the earth, one of each for every day of His creation, having the opposite effect of the good work that He had done. But notice that in the seventh seal, there is silence in heaven, as stated in Revelation 8, symbolizing His seventh day of rest and completion of His work. In like manner, the sound of the seventh trumpet also seems to determine that all has been accomplished, as described in Revelation 11:15–19. And when you read chapter 16, you will as well notice that on the seventh bowl, a voice from heaven says: "It is done," bringing a final rest to God's work as stated in Genesis 2:3 and 4. Can you now see the similarity between the seventh day of God's rest and the last of these events? Were you able to notice that these events are also within an equal number of threes (seals, trumpets, and bowls)?

A Brief Summary of Genesis, Chapter 11 through Chapter 1

In the section below, you will read a brief summary of the chapters that I have described from Genesis 11 through 1, and how closely they relate to the events of these and future end times.

Genesis 11—A story that closely resembles the events of September 11, 2001 (World Trade Center).

Genesis 10—Names of nations that presently are and will be preparing for the ultimate war against Israel as stated in Ezekiel 38 and 39.

Genesis 9—Events that are more frequent now than ever before: drunkenness, homosexuality, murders, and suicides.

Genesis 8—The lawless one who will appear during the time of the worldwide event.

Genesis 6 and 7—The protection that several will receive during the time of the worldwide event as described in Revelation 3:10.

Genesis 4 and 5—The redemption, the Great Tribulation, and the first resurrection of God's people.

Genesis 3—The fall of the serpent that references with the fall of Satan in Revelation 20.

Genesis 1 and 2—What God created in the beginning (Genesis 1 and 2) relates with what will be in the time of the end (Revelation 21 and 22).

Chapter Thirteen

The Judgment:
A Biblical Synopsis

Below I list several Old Testament scriptures of the Bible that give evidence with regard to events that were revealed to the prophets of old, events that will relate to several New Testament scriptures of the Bible, which will be relevant to the Day of Judgment and to His return (rapture).

As you read these passages, notice how these events that are being described seem to correspond to events that are to take place before the coming of the Lord. And as you read Joel 2:31, you will notice that this event was also revealed to the prophet Isaiah (13:10), and can also be referenced with Matthew 24:29, Acts 2:20, and Revelation 6:12. However, notice Amos 5:18, 5:20, Isaiah 13:6, and 13:9, for they describe an event that is called the "Day of the Lord." This day could well represent the day of wrath, but when you read Acts 2:19-20 and relate it with the other passages that are cited throughout this paragraph, I am certain that you will be able to determine that those who desire the day of the Lord do not desire judgment upon themselves, but His arrival (rapture). Therefore, by this determination, I am certain that this phrase "Day of the Lord" is not referring exclusively to the Day of Judgment, as many believe, but also to His coming. So if the prophecies of Joel 2, Isaiah 13, and Amos 5 and 8 relate with the sixth seal of Revelation 6:12, then it is evident that the first six seals of Revelation 6 will eventually take place before the coming of the Lord. But pay close attention to the capitalized words within these passages, for it will give evidence supporting the belief in the events of the Great Tribulation, before the time of His coming.

Joel 2:29–32—And also on My menservants and on My maidservants I will pour out My Spirit in those days. And I will show wonders in the heavens and in the earth: Blood and fire and pillars of smoke. The sun shall be turned into darkness, And the moon into blood, BEFORE the COMING of the great and awesome DAY OF THE LORD. And it shall come to pass that whoever calls on the name of the LORD shall be saved. For in Mount Zion and in Jerusalem there shall be deliverance, as the LORD has said, Among the remnant whom the LORD calls".

Amos 5:16–23—Therefore, thus says the LORD, the God of hosts, the LORD: "In all the squares there shall be wailing, and in all the streets they shall say, 'Alas! Alas!' They shall call the farmers to mourning and to wailing those who are skilled in lamentation, and in all vineyards there shall be wailing, for I will pass through your midst," says the LORD. Woe to you who desire the day of the LORD! WHY WOULD YOU HAVE THE DAY OF THE LORD? It is darkness, and not light, as if a man fled from a lion, and a bear met him, or went into the house and leaned his hand against the wall, and a serpent bit him. Is not the day of the LORD darkness, and not light, and gloom with no brightness in it? I hate, I despise your feasts, and I take no delight in your solemn assemblies. Even though you offer me your burnt offerings and grain offerings, I will not accept them; and the peace offerings of your fattened animals, I will not look upon them. Take away from me the noise of your songs; to the melody of your harps I will not listen.

Amos 8:8–12—Shall not the land tremble on this account, and everyone mourn who dwells in it, and all of it rise like the Nile, and be tossed about and sink again, like the Nile of Egypt? "And on that day," declares the Lord GOD, "I will make the sun go down at noon and darken the earth in broad daylight. I will turn your feasts into mourning and all your songs into lamentation; I will bring sackcloth on every waist and baldness on every head; I will make it like the mourning for an only son and the end of it like a bitter day." "Behold, the days are coming," declares the Lord God, "when I will send a famine on the land—not a famine of bread, nor a thirst for water, but of hearing the words of the LORD. They shall wander from sea to sea, and from north to east; they shall run to and fro, to seek the word of the LORD, but they shall not find it."

Isaiah 13:6-7—Wail, for the DAY OF THE LORD IS AT HAND! It will come as destruction from the Almighty. Therefore all hands will be limp,. . . Every man's heart will melt.

Isaiah 13:9–13—Behold, the DAY OF THE LORD COMES, Cruel, with both wrath and fierce anger, to lay the land desolate; and He will destroy its sinners from it. For the stars of heaven and their constellations will not give their light; the sun will be darkened in its going forth, and the moon will not cause its light to shine. I will punish the world for its evil, and the wicked for their iniquity; I will halt the arrogance of the proud, and will lay low the haughtiness of the terrible. I will make a mortal more rare than fine gold, a man more than the golden wedge of Ophir. Therefore I will shake the heavens, and the earth will move out of her place, In the wrath of the LORD of hosts and in the day of His fierce anger.

Acts 2:19–20—"I will show wonders in heaven above and signs in the earth beneath: Blood and fire and vapor of smoke. The sun shall be turned into darkness, and the moon into blood, BEFORE THE COMING OF THE GREAT AND AWESOME DAY OF THE LORD.

1 Thessalonians 5:1–2—But concerning the times and the seasons, brethren, you have no need that I should write to you. For you yourselves know perfectly that THE DAY OF THE LORD so comes as a thief in the night.

2 Peter 3:1012–But the DAY OF THE LORD will come as a thief in the night, in which the heavens will pass away with a great noise, and the elements will melt with fervent heat; both the earth and the works that are in it will be burned up. Therefore, since all these things will be dissolved, what manner of persons ought you to be in holy conduct and godliness, looking for and hastening the coming of the DAY OF GOD, because of which the heavens will be dissolved, being on fire, and the elements will melt with fervent heat?

Matthew 24:44–Therefore you also be ready, for the Son of Man is COMING at an hour you do not expect.

With regard to the evidence of these passages, can we now truly deny that these disastrous events of tribulation will occur after the time of His coming? CAN ONE BRING FORTH OTHER BIBLICAL EVIDENCE THAT WILL DISPROVE THESE BELIEFS?

Although the seven seals of Revelation 6 were provided as seen below, the main focus OF these seals will be geared toward the events of the fifth and sixth seals, for if you notice, these particular seals, which are spoken of by the prophets, seem to take place before the coming of the Lord.

Furthermore, if you take into account the increasing and unusual events of this present time—economy, murders, suicides, deaths, and so on—they would seem to relate with several of the seals of Revelation 6.

First seal—Rider on white horse went about conquering and to conquer.

Second seal—Rider on the red horse takes peace from the earth that people should kill one another.

Third seal—Black horse: A quart of wheat for a day's wages and three quarts of barley for a day's wages.

Fourth seal—Pale horse: Death and Hades were given power to kill with sword, with hunger, with death, and by the beasts of the earth.

Fifth seal—Souls that were persecuted and slain for the word of God and its testimony.

Sixth seal—A great earthquake, the darkening of the sun, the moon turned blood red, and the stars of heaven fell to the earth.

Seventh seal—There is silence in heaven for about half an hour (the completion of the opening of all seven seals).

In the section of this paragraph, I briefly describe and illustrate the events of the sixth seal, which have led me to believe that the other seals of Revelation 6 will eventually occur before the day of His coming (rapture). For as we look into the events of the sixth seal, we will be able to see that once this seal was opened, a massive earthquake took place, the sun became black as a sackcloth of hair, the moon became like blood, and the stars of heaven fell to the earth, as a fig tree drops its late figs when it is shaken by a mighty wind. As we reference these events with those that are written and spoken of by God's servants in Isaiah 13:10-13, Joel 2:31, Amos 5:18-20, Amos 8:9, Matthew 24:29, Mark 13:24, Luke 21:25, and Acts 2:19-20, it will seem to describe that the events of the sixth seal will take place "Before the COMING of the great and awesome Day of the LORD."

As we now look into Matthew 27, you will see several events that seem to symbolize and relate with the events of the fifth and sixth seals of Revelation 6. Matthew 27:45 describes a darkness that came upon the land during the time of Jesus's persecution (crucifixion). And when you turn to Revelation 6:9, you will see God's people being persecuted and slain before the darkness came upon the earth.

But after Jesus gives up His Spirit in verse 50, an earthquake takes place, in the same manner the earthquake of Revelation 6:12 will come about, after the death of those who had held to the testimony of Christ. But notice that after His death, the darkness, and the earthquake, "the graves were opened; and many bodies of the saints who had fallen asleep were raised; and coming out of the graves after His resurrection, they went into the holy city and appeared to many" (Matthew 27:52 and 53). However, one notable part of this verse, which resembles that of the resurrection is when "many Holy people" (not all) came out of the graves "After His Resurrection," in the same manner as will happen at the time of His coming: persecution of God's people (Revelation 6:9–11), the great earthquake and darkness (Revelation 6:12), then the resurrection of God's chosen people (Revelation 7), just as they took place in Matthew 27:52 and 53 and Revelation 7:9. Aren't we noticing a perfect picture of what is to take place during the time of the opening of these seals before the resurrection? It seems that the verses of Ecclesiastes are giving meaning to the order of these events.

Ecclesiastes 1:9—What has been is what will be, and what has been done is what will be done, and there is nothing new under the sun.

Ecclesiastes 1:10—Is there a thing of which it is said, "See, this is new"? It has been already in the ages before us.

Therefore, if the events of the Sun, Moon, and Stars that are stated in the above passages are relevant to those written in Revelation 6:13 and spoken of by Christ in Matthew 24:29 and Mark 13:24, then be assured that times of tribulation will befall the people of the earth before His coming. Read Matthew 24:15-31 AND 1 Corinthians 15:23.

As you may have well realized, my conclusion rests upon the belief of the church being present during the time of the Great Tribulation before the coming of the Lord (rapture). In spite of this belief, which I held for many years in the hope and expectancy of a pre-tribulation rapture, the conclusion to this determination comes not only from the sparse and weak evidence the church has presented up to the present time, but also from the visions, dreams, and revelations I have received throughout the years in reference to the order of these events. Therefore, I do urge that you, if necessary, reread and carefully look into the evidence of this chapter before denying or rejecting this belief, for your life, both physical and spiritual, will depend on it. And again, read Revelation 22:6, 2 Thessalonians 2:1–4 and reference Revelation 2:10 with Revelation 3:10-11 along with the significant evidence from the many passages I have provided throughout this book. Unless proper evidence can be provided supporting the belief of a pre-tribulation rapture, rather than what many have considered and quoted from 1 Thessalonians 5:9 and Revelation 4:1, I suggest you reassess your beliefs, for beliefs alone, without sufficient facts, are not the means to proven evidence.

1 Thessalonians 5:9–For God did not appoint us to wrath, but to obtain salvation through our Lord Jesus Christ. And again, haven't we seen, heard, or known about good churchgoing people who suffered in one way or another during times of catastrophe?

Revelation 4 :1–After these things I looked, and behold, a door standing open in heaven. And the first voice which I heard was like a trumpet speaking with me, saying, "Come up here, and I will show you things which must take place after this. This verse alone does not necessarily symbolize or represent the taking up (rapture) of God's people, nor should it be accepted as such, even within the order in which the chapters of Revelation are presented. For one biblical verse does not necessarily constitute the answer to any given subject, nor does it provide sufficient grounds for one's belief. And again, study Revelation 14:3-16 in order to understand the proper order of these events.

Although believing in a pre-tribulation, mid-tribulation, or post-tribulation coming of the Lord (rapture) will not necessarily cause a loss of one's salvation, be advised that it may cause one to believe and accept the deception of the deceiver (Antichrist) and eventually bring God's judgment upon you. Read 2 Thessalonians 2:9-12 and Revelation 14:9-10.

Chapter fourteen

Conclusion

This is our time to warn New York City and the rest of the world of the impending Day of Judgment, a day that seems to be drawing closer and closer, a time to call upon the people to repent of their sinful ways and turn to the ways of God. For it is the time to look back on the choices we made, and evaluate the benefits or consequences. It's a time to look at the reflection with regard to all the events that took place in our lives, not only from our victories, but also from our failures; it is a time for understanding and a time for repentance. We know that God always watches over the earth and is always waiting for His people to repent. Have you been reflecting on the limitation of this time?

America, nations, and people of the world, we are now on the verge of facing a calamity of great proportion, and what lurks ahead of us will, without prejudice, affect the people of the world. Leaders and people of all nations, have you acknowledged the doomsday that lurks behind your door? Have you not taken into account the several nations that are presently suffering because of the scarcity of their food supply? The pain, sufferings, and hunger the people, especially the children, of these nations have been facing due to disastrous events, government control, unemployment or from economic hardship are but a few of the causes that have brought calamity, mass riots, and death upon these people. Will New York City—the super financial capital of the world—be exempt from any of these events? The current economic dilemma that is being felt in America and other nations is just a shadow of things to come. Will you be prepared? We've knelt in prayer seeking guidance, yet immediately rejected and denied the message that God has revealed to us. Will the precious lives of your children be sacrificed because of your rejections and unbelief? What can you lose if you prepare? If you don't prepare? And what is gained if you prepare? But what is lost if you don't? A life! The time to do the right thing is now. Let us all get in a right relationship with God and one another now, before it is too late. Remember, this is not about religion, for religion is not the means to your salvation. This is about a personal relationship with Christ, the source to your salvation. And again, read Jeremiah 2:35 and Jeremiah 25:29–32.

Therefore, we must make an effort to live in love, unity, and righteousness, having no deceit, hatred, or wrongful acts against one another, but having compassion and consideration toward everyone, living according to His will to the best of our ability. For the two greatest commandments that were placed upon us in order to obtain a closer assurance of our salvation are: "And you shall Love the Lord your God with all your Heart, with all your Soul, with all your Mind, and with all your Strength," and "You shall Love your neighbor as yourself. There is no other commandment greater than these" (Mark 12:30–31). Also read 1 John 3:11, 1 John 3:14-15, and 1 John 3:23-24.

1 John 3:17-18—But if anyone has the world's goods and sees his brother in need, yet closes his heart against him, how does God's love abide in him? Little children, let us not love in word or talk but in deed and in truth.

It has been and always will be the responsibility of God's people to present the gospel in its true and proper form to anyone and everyone we can. By evangelizing to the people, we can increase the possibility of our nation coming together to know the true Messiah. We as children of God are called to bring God's word in its truth, but the problem today is that very little in Christianity and other true religions are of the quality to provoke anyone to anything. Our witness is a powerful one and Satan would like nothing more than to destroy it. Thousands are being deceived and misled by unbiblical messages and false religions every day, and though certain religions believe they are the chosen and true doctrine over all doctrines, the true gospel is that which is preached by those who bring it in the name of Jesus Christ from its original and unedited text. But we should be ashamed of ourselves every time a cult member knocks on our door, or we see two clean-cut boys on bicycles working a neighborhood. They are more zealous for a lie than most of us are for the truth. We have no excuse; it is the sign of the times, the age we are living in right now, the age of the great commission, the age just prior to the coming judgment upon the earth and the calling away of God's chosen believers. Read Mark 12:33.

1 Peter 4:17–19—For it is time for judgment to begin at the household of God; and if it begins with us, what will be the outcome for those who do not obey the gospel of God? And "If the righteous is scarcely saved, what will become of the ungodly and the sinner?" Therefore let those who suffer according to God's will entrust their souls to a faithful Creator while doing good.

Our lives hang in the balance of time and in the hands of God, and no one can be certain of tomorrow. Yes, we will all go sometime, and after we breathe our last breath it is very important where we go, for the crucial fact is not the way in which we go but what our final destination will be. It is of the essence for you to decide whether you would like to accept Jesus Christ into your life or continue your life without Him, for 1 John 5:12 states, "whoever has the Son has life; whoever does not have the Son of God does not have life." 1 John 5:13 states, "I write these things to you who believe in the name of the Son of God that you may know that you have eternal life." The only difference is in Christ, for in Christ we have hope and are able to obtain life even after death, but without Him, our sins still remain, there will be no hope, and being separated from God will be inevitable. Again, you must recognize that our ways may not be

God's ways since it states in Proverbs 16:25, "there is a way that seems right to a man, but its end is the way to death" (death meaning being in separation from God). Also in Matthew 12:30 it states, "Whoever is not with Me is against Me, and whoever does not gather with Me scatters." Also read John 3:36.

1 Thessalonians 5:20-22—Do not despise prophecies. Test all things; hold fast what is good. Abstain from every form of evil.

Revelation 22:6-7—Then he said to me, "These words are faithful and true. And the Lord God of the holy prophets sent His angel to show His servants the things which must shortly take place." "Behold, I am coming quickly! Blessed is he who keeps the words of the prophecy of this book."

As I close this chapter, I ask that God may enlighten you in the wisdom of His word as you reflect upon the contents of this book, for it was intended to bring light upon your life, not as a means to confuse, but to help and protect you within the love of Christ.

May the grace of our Lord Jesus Christ be with you all. Amen.

Printed in the United States
214703BV00001B/7/P

9 781605 309583